TRAIL RUNNING ILLUSTRATED

THE ART OF RUNNING FREE

Doug Mayer and Brian Metzler

**MOUNTAINEERS
BOOKS**

RECURRING ICONS WE'LL USE:

NERD ALERT

SAFETY ISSUE!

THE WONDERFUL WORLD
OF TRAIL RUNNING

OPINION AHEAD

IT'S SCIENCE!

TAKE IT TO THE
NEXT LEVEL

WE LEARNED
THIS ONE
THE HARD WAY

Contents

INTRODUCTION

It was late in my long run, walking up a steep section of trail, water bottles almost empty, legs encrusted with dirt I'd kicked up, when I stepped aside to let two downhill-bound mountain bikers pass. They thanked me, and the second one said, "Enjoy your hike" as he pedaled off. I immediately wanted to protest, as I had already run 30-something kilometers that day, and was dressed like a runner: running shoes, running shorts, weird-looking running vest carrying all my water and food for the day. How dare this person mistake me for a . . . hiker?

I continued uphill, keeping a fast pace the last 100 or so meters to the top of my final climb of the day, where I would start running again, and I thought: "Enjoy your hike." Based on the ratio of time spent running to time spent walking that day, that guy was about 30 to 40 percent correct. I hike the uphills, I run everything else. I call it "trail running" because it's faster than hiking, and I take way less stuff with me, but I see the same scenery I'd see if I hiked, just more quickly.

And I love moving fast on trails—fast, for me, anyway. Sure, you have to look down a lot more often than when you run on a road, keeping your eye out for rocks and roots, but you get to look up a lot, too, and the view is always changing. You see wildlife. You find a rhythm, bouncing down the trail, and lose yourself in thought for minutes at a time. You never cross a street, never have to watch out for cars, and maybe most importantly, never have to frantically find a public restroom in the middle of a city when a gurgly stomach turns into a hurricane of desperation. You get ups and downs, turns and switchbacks in the trail, keeping you from getting too bored.

When I think about trail running memories, only a few minutes total of the hundreds of hours I've spent on trails stick out—a wildlife sighting here and there, a few sunsets, the way the light filtered through the trees on a particular late-fall afternoon. The memories are mostly tonal: the general calm that I always feel after about 50 minutes of moving through the forest or in the mountains, the everything's-going-to-be-OK glow of endorphins from working hard, and the general feel of a few trail sections I've run dozens of times. Even with a vest full of 40-kilometers' worth of water and food, I still feel light, free, and fast (though, yes, the occasional mountain biker mistakes me for a hiker).

That light, free, fast feeling is probably the best reason I've found to run on trails. Of course, there are plenty of other reasons, which you'll discover as you work your way through this book. The point of a book like this, to me, is a) to answer your questions (some of which you didn't know you had), and b) make you feel like putting the book down, slipping your feet into some shoes, and going for a run, whether it's 5 km or 50 km. So enjoy this book, and when you set it down, enjoy all those hours of trail running that will no doubt follow.

Brendan Leonard, founder of Semi-Rad.com

You're off to Great Places,
Today is your day!
Your mountain is waiting,
So ... get on your way!

Dr. Seuss, *Oh, the Places You'll Go!*

CHAPTER 1

ONCE UPON A TIME

Once upon a time, before written history, there was a trail run to the top of a mountain. The story goes that thousands of years ago, the Irish hero Fionn mac Cumhaill was very much in demand with the ladies. Fionn organized a trail run, and the fastest woman to the top of the hill on which he stood would become his partner. So, it could just be that the first known trail run was a women's trail race held in the name of love.

The Irish myth continues that Fionn, already in love with Gráinne, showed her a shortcut. She won the race. It is lost to history as to whether any of the other competitors complained, but this may also be the first recorded case of collusion between a race director and a runner. (Love will do things like that.) Today, the mountain is called *Slievenamon*, which translates as "mountain of the fair women."

Trail running began long before that, of course—less for love and more out of necessity. Two million years ago, our ancestors evolved from living in trees to running on two feet. We ran through forests, over mountains, and across savannas, chasing prey that would become dinner. We developed specific features —longer legs, springlike tendons, and feet that absorb impact— so we could run long distances. We became expert trail runners, so much so that to this day, we are still built to outrun horses and antelope over long distances.

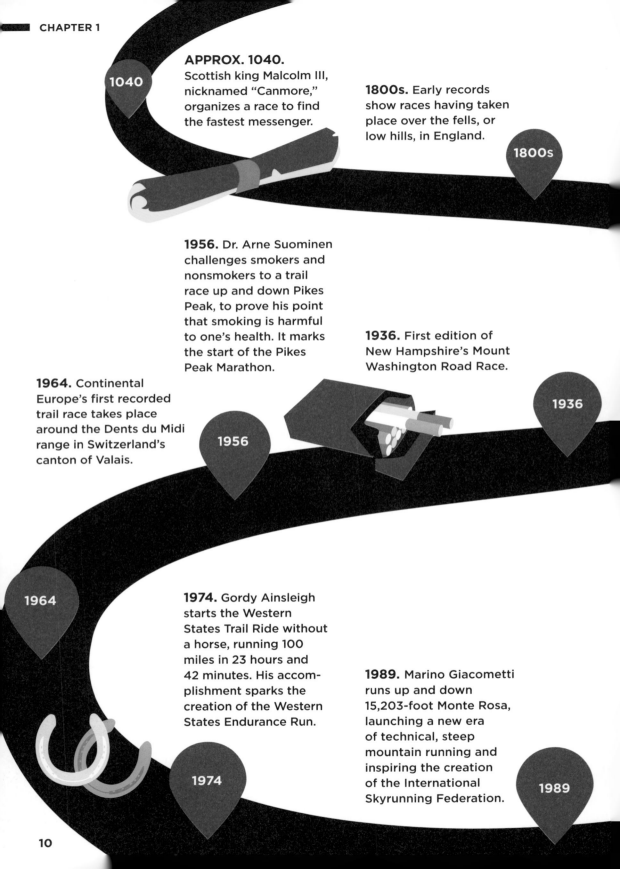

APPROX. 1040. Scottish king Malcolm III, nicknamed "Canmore," organizes a race to find the fastest messenger.

1040

1800s. Early records show races having taken place over the fells, or low hills, in England.

1800s

1956. Dr. Arne Suominen challenges smokers and nonsmokers to a trail race up and down Pikes Peak, to prove his point that smoking is harmful to one's health. It marks the start of the Pikes Peak Marathon.

1936. First edition of New Hampshire's Mount Washington Road Race.

1936

1964. Continental Europe's first recorded trail race takes place around the Dents du Midi range in Switzerland's canton of Valais.

1956

1964

1974. Gordy Ainsleigh starts the Western States Trail Ride without a horse, running 100 miles in 23 hours and 42 minutes. His accomplishment sparks the creation of the Western States Endurance Run.

1989. Marino Giacometti runs up and down 15,203-foot Monte Rosa, launching a new era of technical, steep mountain running and inspiring the creation of the International Skyrunning Federation.

1974

1989

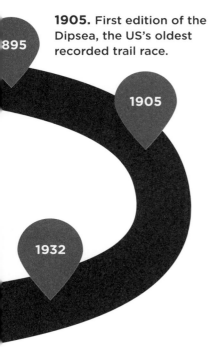

1895. First trail race up the Scottish mountain Ben Nevis.

1905. First edition of the Dipsea, the US's oldest recorded trail race.

895

1905

1932

1932. Bob Graham breaks England's Lakeland Fell record, crossing 42 fells in under 24 hours.

A FEW MILEPOSTS IN THE HISTORY OF TRAIL RUNNING

Trail running is no longer a necessity for love or survival. (Though we're guessing love still sometimes plays a role!) In their place, trail running for recreation rules the day. The sport is currently experiencing rapid growth. Around the world, runners are moving from the roads to the trails. In doing so, they are experiencing the unique qualities of an activity that returns us to our roots, provides numerous health benefits, and when the last steps have been taken, leaves in its wake a sense of calm that comes with moving quietly through nature. The timing could not be better. In a society where the crush of work and technology feels omnipresent, we need trail running now more than ever.

Like our ancestors, we already own everything we need to trail run. We've made a few improvements over the years, of course—comfortable shoes, convenient vests, gear to cope with challenging environments. We've learned a thing or two as well. This book will bring beginners up to speed on everything you need to know to get you on your way. For the experienced trail runner, you'll find valuable tips and insights that will improve your trail running. Enjoy—and happy trail running!

2003. First running of the Ultra-Trail du Mont-Blanc, starting and finishing in Chamonix, France. Today, UTMB is the world's most famous trail race. 10,000 runners take part in one of seven events at the end of August each year.

2003

Why Trail Run?

Think back to when you were a kid. Before you had toys, games, and rules to follow. How did you play? Chances are, you ran through a park, or on a beach, or maybe even in a forest.

Trail running is the original form of play.

When we trail run—hopping over rocks, diving full-speed down hills, weaving around trees in a forest—we relive those moments. Play, one of the freest expressions of ourselves, is reason enough to trail run. But there are many others. Here are a few of our favorites.

IT'S JUST PLAIN FUN

There are moments when trail running is hard, even painful. There are times when it's frustrating. But most of the time, it's just plain fun. When else can grown adults jump off boulders while yelling, "Yippee!"?

WE GET TO EXPLORE OUTSIDE

So much of our lives is spent indoors. Trail running takes you outside and allows you to strike out into new territory.

FITNESS

Trail running is a well-rounded form of exercise, building aerobic fitness, muscle strength, and endurance.

MENTAL HEALTH

Run along a trail, and you'll find that the weight of the world slowly disappears from your shoulders. Trail running, with its ever-changing terrain, requires more concentration than other forms of running. That steady focus is relaxing, perhaps not too different from meditation. Problems seem less burdensome, and sometimes solutions even come to mind.

CHALLENGE AND GROWTH

Trail running offers a challenge to everyone, no matter your level. When we trail run, we often find ourselves stepping out of our comfort zone, whether we are taking our first steps in a new activity or running a 100-mile race. That challenge is a form of personal growth, providing a sense of fulfillment and satisfaction.

INCLUSIVENESS

Trail running is often seen as something only for uber-fit mountain jocks. The truth is, anyone can trail run, and all kinds of people do. Trail runners come in all shapes and sizes, and cross all sorts of boundaries.

MEET KILIAN, THE WORLD'S MOST INCREDIBLE TRAIL RUNNER

Kilian Jornet, from the Catalonia region of Spain, may be the strongest trail runner ever.

Jornet holds course records at tough, highly competitive races around the world. He is a seven-time world champion in Skyrunning, a type of trail racing that includes extremely steep and challenging mountain terrain. He has won Colorado's Hardrock 100 four times, is a three-time international ultrarunning champion, and has won Chamonix, France's prestigious Ultra-Trail du Mont-Blanc three times, too.

But Jornet does much more than just trail race. He has set speed records on some of the world's most iconic peaks, logging "Fastest Known Times" on Mount Everest, Mont Blanc, Denali, and the Matterhorn. By blurring the lines between technical climbing and trail running, he has fundamentally changed the idea of what's possible. For these accomplishments, National Geographic named Jornet Adventurer of the Year in both 2014 and 2018.

Jornet is also one of the world's best ski mountaineering racers, with accolades that include five Vertical Race World Champion titles and 30 podiums at World Cup events.

He is famous for his tough training regimen and has one of the highest VO2 max scores ever recorded: 92 ml/kg/min. The VO2 max number is a scientific measure of how well your body uses oxygen, and therefore is a good indicator of your performance in endurance sports.

Jornet was raised in a mountain hut in Spain's Pyrenees mountains, where his father was the hut caretaker and mountain guide. At age five, he climbed Aneto, the highest peak in the Pyrenees. By age 15, he had already earned a spot on the Spanish national ski mountaineering team as a junior member.

Kilian Jornet lives in a remote mountainous region of Norway, where he trains with his partner and fellow trail runner and ski mountaineer, Emelie Forsberg, and their Labradoodle, Maui.

TAKE IT NEXT LEVEL

There's a mile you run before you even start sweating. Norwegian runners have a concept they call *dørmile*. Literally, it translates as **"the door mile."** The door mile is the mental and physical distance you travel from the time you want to go for a run to the time your trail running shoes hit dirt. Norwegians consider it the hardest of all the miles, because it requires overcoming inertia. The next time you're trail running with a friend, and you're about to start moving, high-five each other—you both just ticked off the *dørmile*!

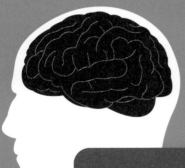

THIS IS YOUR BRAIN ON TRAIL RUNNING

Our modern lives, with a hectic work pace and a constant online connection, can leave us feeling fried. Trail running relieves that mental exhaustion. You'll feel calmer and more centered after a good trail run for good reason—your brain is literally healing. University of Utah researcher David Strayer has been studying the connection between time spent in the outdoors and the health of our brains. "Being in nature allows the prefrontal cortex, the brain's command center, to dial down and rest," says Strayer. "Like an overused muscle."

CHAPTER 2

RUNNING ON TRAILS

In this chapter, we'll share some tips for making your trail running even better. You'll learn ways to improve your form so you run more efficiently and avoid injury.

You might even find yourself sharing some of the same feelings other trail runners expressed when we asked them what words came to mind when they thought about trail running. Their choices? Adventurous, liberating, inspiring. And—oh, yes— muddy, too!

You Already Know How to Trail Run

That's right. You already know how to trail run.

So, before you read this, here's our suggestion: read the following list, then put down this book and go for a run on the nearest trail you can find. With luck, there's a park not too very far away. We've been running for two million years, so it should feel pretty natural!

Here are our tips to help get you started:

1. Grab a friend. It's always great to share a new experience with someone. And when you're each running your first trail race, you can reminisce together!

2. Send someone a text that you're going on a trail run and tell them where you're starting and when you'll be back. Besides being a good habit to get into, you'll feel cool.

3. Lose your expectations. Trail running is different from any other kind of running you've ever done. Don't be afraid to walk!

4. Pick a trail without much steep climbing or descending. Rolling hills are one thing, but avoid a lot of vertical gain, or big "vert," when you can.

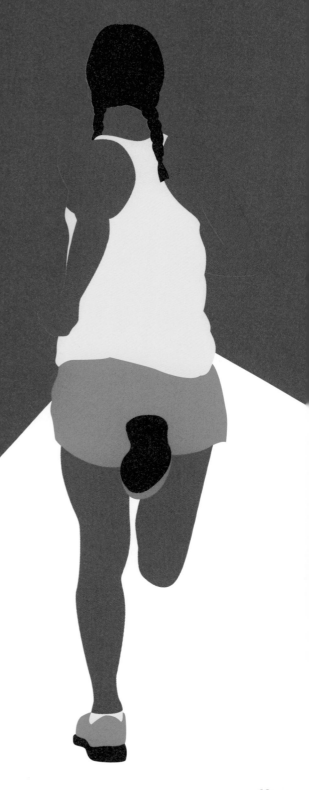

5. If you're used to running on roads, find a trail that's no more than half the distance of what you usually run on roads. Trail running is typically harder (and slower) than road running!

6. Pick a trail with a smooth surface and as few rocks and roots as possible.

7. Leave your watch at home, and if you use an app like Strava on your phone, leave it off. Forget about goals for your first couple of trail runs. Why? See #3.

8. Trail running is a contact sport. Don't worry about it. You might fall. You might get a cut and you might get bruised. The trail might even draw blood! It happens—and it's normal. Even the best trail runners fall occasionally.

9. Don't worry too much about the gear, either. You're going on a very short run. Even though there are great reasons to use a trail-specific running shoe, your regular running shoes should suffice for this short run. If it's sunny, a running cap, sunglasses, and sunblock are all you'll really need.

10. Go at a quiet time when trails aren't crowded so you won't be self-conscious. Don't sweat your pace, and make sure you stop and take in the scenery at least once.

11. Congratulate yourself. You're out pushing your boundaries, and that's a good thing! Well done for lacing them up.

12. If this list is too long for you, remember this: trail running is instinctive. There's a lot you'll be doing right already.

13. Don't forget to smile. Studies show it will make your run feel easier— no kidding!

You'll want to listen to your body carefully as you get started. It will take some time to warm up and get into a groove. As you run, feel the dirt and rocks under your feet. What sounds do you hear? Check out the views as you run, stopping if you need to. Keep an eye out for wildlife. Notice how your gait and body position change with the terrain. In short, pay attention.

Okay, here's where you put the book down and run. Have fun out there!

How'd it go? Here's a collection of words we crowdsourced from trail runners, describing their trail runs. Which ones apply to you?

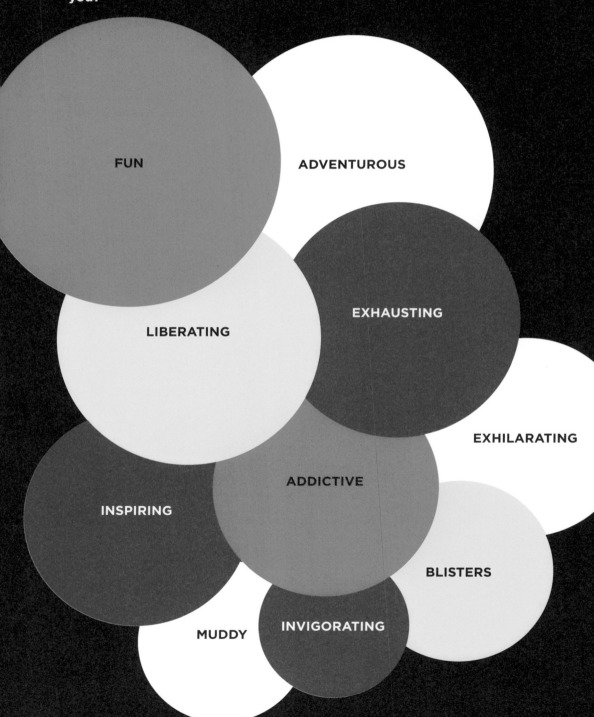

FUN

ADVENTUROUS

LIBERATING

EXHAUSTING

EXHILARATING

INSPIRING

ADDICTIVE

BLISTERS

MUDDY

INVIGORATING

CLUMSY

VIEWS

REBELLIOUS

MEDITATIVE

FREEING

HAPPY

JOYFUL

ENLIGHTENING

STEEP

LIFE-CHANGING

IN THE ZONE

HUMBLING

WOW

HARD

AWAKENING

REVEALING

FLYING

SURPRISING

TRANS-CENDENT

MAGICAL

BREATHLESS

AWAKENED

FREE

UH OH

Describe your first trail run:

1. It was harder than I thought it would be because of the hills.
2. I tripped a few times on the rocks and scraped my leg on some bushes.
3. I enjoyed the scenery, noticed some flowers, and saw some wildlife.
4. It really felt good when I finished and I plan to head to another trail soon.
5. All of the above.

We're guessing you picked #5! (And if not, that at least a few of the items in this list were true.) Nearly every trail run is a great adventure and a lot of fun.

Congrats on ticking off your first trail run! Keep reading. In the pages ahead, we'll add to what you now know about running on trails.

Tackling the Technique

There is a certain beauty to the simplicity of trail running. You don't need much gear, and running is something we've each known how to do since not long after we first stood up and started walking.

Though it's part of our DNA, it helps to understand exactly what's happening with our bodies when we run on trails. With that knowledge comes the ability to make corrections, improve our skills, and become better, more capable trail runners.

RUN TALL AND TURN IT OVER FAST

Imagine what your form looks like when you run fast. What do you see? For most people, the first thing that subconsciously suggests speed is quick turnover of their feet, also known as a high cadence. The strides are soft and quick, with a strong rear-ward kick. The person is running tall, with good posture and arms held close to the body. Most of all, he or she looks relaxed.

With trail running, smooth is fast. Your goal is to minimize wasted effort, dancing over rocks and roots like a mountain goat and motoring over flats like a gazelle. In other words, it's all about reducing the amount of energy you're using, no matter the terrain. Let's dig into the nitty-gritty of how to make that happen, starting with your feet.

TOUCHDOWN!

Let's overturn a misconception: there is no ideal place on your foot to first make ground contact, or "foot-strike." Some trail runners swear by running on their toes and others on their midfeet, but all that really matters is where your feet strike the ground in relation to your center of gravity. The key is to avoid overstriding by having your feet land under the midline of your hips, rather than slightly in front of that midline.

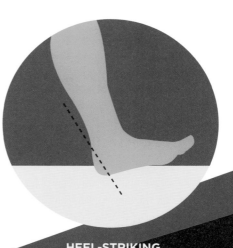

HEEL-STRIKING

Your body naturally wants to maximize the surface area underfoot at impact. For many runners, that means a mid-foot strike. Heel-striking is often associated with overstriding. Toe-striking is active, rather than passive, requiring a pointed foot that uses additional energy.

To achieve the ideal landing, relax your feet and ankles and take short strides, so that your feet land directly under your center of gravity. Where your feet land will depend on whether you're going uphill or downhill, but the result will be ideal for your physiology.

When in doubt, aim for shorter strides. You'll be more stable, since each footfall will be under your center of gravity, allowing you to more easily adjust your balance. Shorter strides also mean less force when your foot hits the ground—and that can mean fewer injuries.

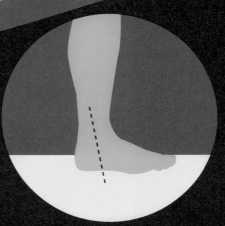

MIDLINE-STRIKING

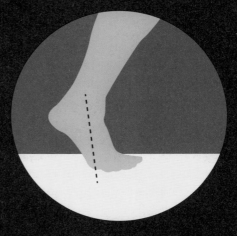

TOE-STRIKING

STRIDE RIGHT

Trail running geeks talk about "stride dynamics," which are nothing more than a set of choices you make as you run. Here are two key points to keep in mind as you move forward:

1. Your stride should be soft. Listen to your footfall when running. Does it sound like a light pitter-patter, or like a linebacker playing a set of bongo drums? Ideally, you are quiet enough that you can sneak up on someone like a ninja!

2. Your stride should be quick, even if the varied terrain doesn't always allow you to stride consistently. This distributes load more efficiently and allows you to be more nimble on the trail. It might feel odd at first, but you'll get the hang of it. Remember your goal: short, rapid strides.

RELAX YOUR HIPS AND PRACTICE GOOD POSTURE

If you want to impress your trail running partner, you can call this "glute engagement." For our purposes, though, the best way to think about this concept is to focus on relaxing your hips and practicing good posture. Here are three steps to remember:

1. Stand up straight. If you're like most people, your hip flexors will be tight. Relax and loosen them, activating your glutes slightly. Now, move your hips forward. Your spine should straighten. That's it!

2. Take this relaxed-hip-flexor posture to the trail. When running, think about flowing back, rather than pulling forward. The moment of power in your running motion is when your foot pushes off the ground behind your body; maximizing push-off comes from relaxed hip flexors that allow a full range of motion, not a flexed butt.

3. To really understand glute engagement, familiarize yourself with strides. "Striding," in this context, doesn't mean taking a few steps. Sometimes called "striders," "stride-outs," or "accelerations," each stride is an acceleration covering about 100 meters, and taking 20–30 seconds.

4. Now, try a fast set of strides on a slight downhill. The best downhill runners have mastered that relaxed-hip-flexor, flowing-back running form. While accelerating, try to stay relaxed and get as close to top speed as possible without sprinting. That's it! Now try to keep that form up as much as possible, including at slower paces and on variable terrain.

KICK IT BACK

The rearward flow through push-off is most evident in elite road runners, who usually have a strong back kick. Recreational runners, on the other hand, look like they are riding a bike, with pronounced forward motion.

ARM SWING

Let's dispel another myth: Swinging your arms excessively doesn't help propel you forward. Instead, it counteracts the motion in your hips and the drive of your legs that help your body stay balanced.

The most efficient way to hold your arms when running is to keep them close to your body.

Now, focus on keeping your arm angle compact, at 90 degrees or less throughout the arm swing. In other words, if you draw a line from your shoulder to your elbow to your wrist, it should form a right angle. Don't let your arm angle open up, or you'll lose efficiency.

THINK LIKE A T-REX

Top runners often form short levers with their arms, sometimes around 70 degrees. By keeping the angle at 90 degrees or less, their arm swing uses less energy, which can then be used where it's really needed—in the legs. So think like a T-Rex: keep your arms next to your body. Do that, and you'll be one step closer to Velociraptor speeds.

No need to overdo it, by the way. You can and should let your arms extend laterally to the sides to help you keep your balance on the trails—much the way some animals use their tails to keep their balance.

Here's a bonus tip about arm position: If you are trail running with a big, fancy GPS watch, or holding something in one or both of your hands, be aware that it can alter how you hold your arms, which will alter your arm movement—and, therefore, the rest of your movement.

Making Steady Progress

Good form takes time, so you'll need to be patient. When you trail run, you'll be mixing up your stride, using different techniques on different types of trails and across different sections. Don't get discouraged, just enjoy each moment.

If you find yourself stressing over your form, our advice is this: *just run.* Embrace what makes you unique as a trail runner. Your form can be dirty and messy just like the trails. The point is to have fun, and we hope you'll be smiling as you cruise through the countryside, even if you think you're more tortoise than hare. Test the running principles in this chapter, then find the form that works for you. Whatever you choose to do, don't sweat the details. The important thing is to have fun as you run!

DIFFERENT STRIDES FOR DIFFERENT FOLKS

US ultrarunner Courtney Dauwalter is one of the most successful trail runners ever. "I've filmed her a lot. She bounces across the landscape. It's not the most graceful form, but it gets the job done better than anyone else," says trail running filmmaker and artist Max Romey.

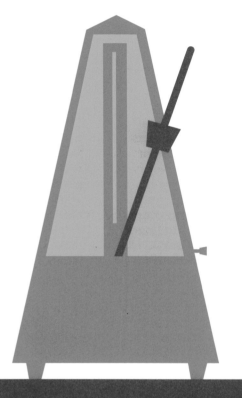

TAKING IT NEXT LEVEL: COUNT YOUR CADENCE

If you want to get really geeky, target a running cadence that works for you. To find out your stride rate, count how many times your right leg hits the ground in 30 seconds, then multiply by four. If you want to experiment with different stride rates, use a metronome track, which is easily available from streaming services like Spotify and YouTube. Many elite runners come in at around 180 strides per minute, but keep in mind that your pace at any given time, along with the ever-changing terrain—uphills, downhills, rocks, roots, puddles, mud, stream crossings, etc.—will affect your cadence.

And don't sweat it too much if you're an outlier, either! American trail running superstar Jim Walmsley is well-known for his loping stride rate of about 165.

TIPS AND TRICKS FOR BETTER FORM

1. Run tall. Consciously focus on running with the top of your head as high as you can get it, without bouncing in your stride.

2. Touch your chest. Try to run while keeping your hands close to your pectoral muscles throughout your arm swings. That may be a little bit too close in practice, but the effort is a good reminder to not open up the angle at your elbow.

3. Thrust at speed. Try to move your hips as far forward as possible and lean forward a little bit. This trick will keep you from "sitting down" or "getting into the backseat" with your running form, which is inefficient.

    Warning: You might feel like you strapped a rocket to your back!

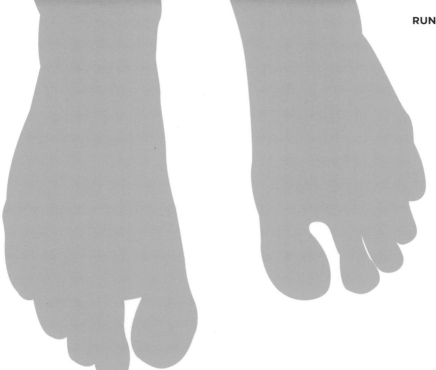

4. Try 180. Using either the cadence-counting or metronome method on page 31, see what it feels like to run at a cadence of 180—or as high as you can comfortably go—for about a half mile. Maintain that cadence, and observe how running with a soft, quick stride affects your perceived level of exertion.

5. Run barefoot on grass. The best way to practice proper stride dynamics is to take your shoes off and run barefoot on soft grass. Your body will naturally adjust to soft, quick strides under your center of gravity because there is no reason for your body to land on your heels for protection. Added bonus: fresh grass feels great under your feet!

CHAPTER 3

GEARING UP

Unlike many outdoor sports, trail running doesn't need to be gear intensive. You can head out on a short trail run with as little as a good pair of shoes, a pair of shorts, and a T-shirt.

Many trail runners will eventually become "gear geeks," obsessed with the latest shoes, apparel, hydration packs, and more. However, there's no need to max out your credit card just yet. Not everyone needs to be a trail running nerd with a truckload of gear.

The longer and farther you go, though, the more you'll want gear to help make the journey comfortable and safe. Let's take a look at some of the key items you'll want to consider.

How About Some Shoes?

Although a few diehard barefoot runners find shoes optional, here's the reality: for the rest of us, our trail running shoes are the most important piece of gear for this activity.

Deciding which shoe is right for you comes down to which models fit your feet the best and what type of terrain you run on most frequently. Try on as many different kinds of shoes as you can before you buy a pair. You'll learn which ones work best for your feet over different terrain, and at various speeds and distances.

Trail running shoes offer some key features that road running shoes lack. Here's what to look for:

KNOBBY OUTSOLE TREAD
(called "lugs") give you traction, especially on wet, muddy terrain.

A "ROCK PLATE"
built into the midsole helps protect your feet from rocks and roots.

LATERAL SUPPORT
can help keep you from rolling your ankle.

TIGHTLY WOVEN MESH UPPERS
keep dirt and debris out.

REINFORCED TOE BUMPERS
protect against stubbed toes.

WATERPROOF UPPERS
(sometimes water-resistant) help keep your feet dry on wet or muddy trails.

HEY, TODD, YOU FORGOT YOUR SHOES!

Todd Byers, from Seattle, Washington, has run barefoot for nearly twenty years, on roads and trails. He has run more than 120 marathons without shoes. When asked about the hardest part of barefoot running, he responded, "Using the porta-potties at events!"

GET A GOOD FIT

One of the most important shoe-buying considerations is fit. Always try on shoes before buying them, ideally testing them on a short jog or treadmill run while climbing and descending. Look for a fit that's snug through the midfoot but offers some wiggle room for your toes. When you run uphill, your heels shouldn't rub up and down against the backs of the shoes. On downhills, your toes shouldn't slam into the fronts. If you're on the fence, go with the larger size. Your feet can swell a bit during long or hot runs.

There are many factors to consider when buying a trail running shoe. These include:

LUGS
The deeper the tread on the shoe's outsole, the more muck it can handle. Shallower lugs are better suited to dry or hard-packed trails.

SHOE WEIGHT
This is largely a matter of personal preference. Lighter shoes feel more agile and fast. Heavier shoes can provide more stability for bigger runners or those seeking protection on technical terrain.

STACK HEIGHT
This refers to the total "height" of the shoe under your foot. Generally, the higher the stack height, the more cushioned it will feel. Heavier runners and runners tackling longer distances may appreciate greater stack height. A warning, though: the taller you go, the harder it is to "feel" the the trail under your feet, which can lead to more wipe-outs. Proceed with caution.

HEEL-TO-TOE OFFSET
Now we're getting nerdy! This is the difference between the stack height in the heel and the stack height in the forefoot. "Zero-drop" or low-drop (2–4 mm) shoes more closely mimic barefoot running, whereas the more traditional 8–12 mm drop offers extra cushioning, which can be especially good for "heel strikers"—runners who land on their heels.

LACING SYSTEMS
While most trail running shoes have traditional laces, some shoes feature single-pull "quick laces" or dial closures, which each allow for faster on/off and on-the-go adjustments.

PROTECT YOUR FEET!

The soles, cushioning, and stitching on trail running shoes take a lot of abuse. Keep track of the distance they've traveled and aim to retire them after 300 to 500 miles (500 to 800 km). Don't wait until your old shoes are totally worn out to change to a new pair. Instead, transition gently, alternating pairs of shoes. This is particularly important if you're changing to a new model of shoe. Your feet will thank you!

300–500 MILES

JARGON ALERT

Trail runners love to get nerdy about shoes. It makes a certain amount of sense. It all starts with your feet, and finding the right shoes for *you* can help you avoid injuries as you log long distances on trails.

Here's some jargon you'll hear. Knowing a bit about these terms will help you avoid an awkward answer when your local trail geek texts, "R U a minimalist?"

THE GREAT DEBATE: MAXIMALIST VS. MINIMALIST

There are two different views about the kinds of shoes that are best for trail running. Minimalist shoes are typically lightweight with a low stack height and minimal heel-to-toe drop for a "close-to-ground" feel that mimics barefoot running. This ability to feel the ground will allow you to be more agile on technical terrain. What's lost? Protection from cushioning, toe bumpers, and rock plates in the midsole.

Maximalist shoes typically feature greater stack height for a super-cushy ride that can feel like running on marshmallows. After a long run, your legs will feel less fatigued. On the downside, these shoes tend to be a bit heavier, and you'll lose the precision of more minimalist footwear. This can make running on technical, rocky terrain more challenging.

NEUTRAL CUSHIONED VS. STABILITY VS. MOTION CONTROL . . . HUH?

All of these terms come down to one word: *pronation*, which doesn't describe trail runners who wave their country's flag. It denotes the natural inward roll of your foot with each step.

If you come from road running, you might have heard that too much or too little pronation can result in injury. As a result, many road running shoes are designed to manage pronation.

Pronation isn't an issue in trail running, partly because most trail shoes are more stable than road shoes and also because almost every footstep is different as you trail run. Also, trails are a more forgiving surface than pavement. That softness can offer some protection against injury. If you're a trail runner, you don't need to worry as much about pronation when you're choosing your shoes.

Don't Overlook the Socks

SLIGHTLY DISTURBING BUT TRUE

Our feet can produce up to 2 cups (0.5 L) of sweat *per day*. A good pair of socks can play a key role in keeping our feet dry, happy, and blister-free.

HERE'S WHAT TO LOOK FOR:

MATERIAL
Look for moisture-wicking synthetics or lightweight merino wool.

FIT
Try socks on to ensure a comfortable fit with no excess fabric bunching anywhere.

LENGTH
Midlength or crew socks better shield against trail debris than short socks.

DOUBLE-LAYER
Double-layer socks reduce friction. They're a good choice if your feet are prone to blisters.

COLOR
White socks are fine if you run on roads or a treadmill, but not on the trails. Use them on trails and you'll wind up with ground-in rings around your ankles from the dirt en route.

TOE SOCKS
Some socks have individual toe pockets, which generally offer a slightly cooler feel (think gloves vs. mittens) and can help if you tend to get blisters between your toes.

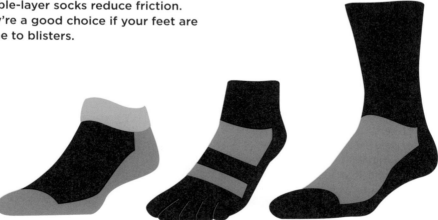

Let's Get Dressed

So far, all you're wearing are your trail running shoes. That's awkward. It's time to get dressed for the trails!

HERE ARE SOME FACTORS TO KEEP IN MIND:

TEMPERATURE

Dress so that you're never shivering, but also beware of overdressing; running turns on your body's furnace and generates a lot of heat—especially when you're running up hills or along mountain trails. This can cause your base layers to get sweaty—a recipe for discomfort. On the flip side, in extreme heat, opt for ultralight, airy clothing to keep cool.

HUMIDITY

The more humid the climate, the more important it is to wear moisture-wicking materials that pull moisture away from your skin and help speed evaporation.

FABRIC

Synthetic materials like nylon or polyester offer excellent insulation and moisture management. Unfortunately, they often get stinky and remain so even after washing. If this is a concern for you, try merino wool. Wool doesn't hold odors, and it still offers good moisture management.

CHAFING

This can be a big concern, especially if you sweat a lot. Experiment liberally and try out new clothing on short runs. Tights or compression shorts, similar to cycling shorts, can be the path to chafe-free bliss. Applying a skin lubricant can also be a big help.

VISIBILITY

If you plan to run on or near roads, especially at dawn, dusk, or dark, wear outer layers that include some reflective materials, so drivers see you. If you're running on trails during hunting season in your area, visibility is super important—in particular, look for "blaze orange" vests or caps so you're not mistaken for an in-season target!

ONE THING TO BRING

A super-lightweight windbreaker that fits in a large pocket, running belt, or pack is one of our favorite items to bring along on a run. Look for one that is water-resistant and hooded, zips into its own pocket, and is small enough that you don't hesitate to carry it.

PRE-OWNED, LOW MILES!

Comfortable clothing can make or break your run. If you're not sure what's right for you . . . experiment! Outdoor clothing can be pricey, but it's getting easier to buy used gear. Both REI and Patagonia offer second-hand goods for sale online, and many retailers are adding a section for lightly-used gear. There are Facebook groups, too, and in the US the website OfferUp is a platform dedicated to selling used items locally.

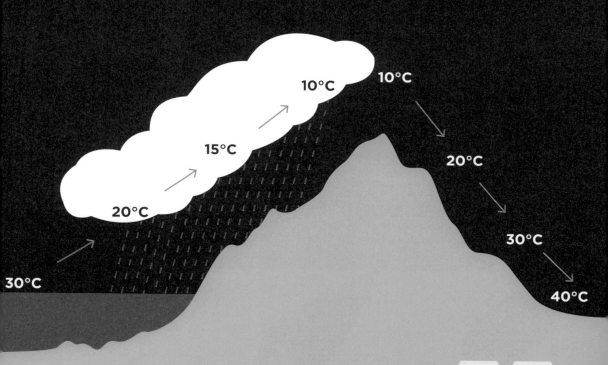

ADIABATIC LAPSE RATE (SAY WHAT?)

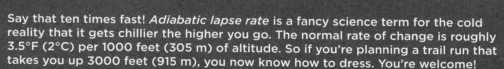

Say that ten times fast! *Adiabatic lapse rate* is a fancy science term for the cold reality that it gets chillier the higher you go. The normal rate of change is roughly 3.5°F (2°C) per 1000 feet (305 m) of altitude. So if you're planning a trail run that takes you up 3000 feet (915 m), you now know how to dress. You're welcome!

WATERPROOF VS. WATER-RESISTANT OUTERWEAR

Lightweight, weather-resistant jackets and pants provide important protection when the weather gets ugly. Some jackets and pants offer fully waterproof protection, whereas others offer just wind and water resistance. Which is best for your needs?

Choose water-resistant if you primarily need wind protection and an emergency shield against light rain or a short, fast-moving storm, or if you're just out for a short run.

Choose waterproof if you'll be running in very heavy rain and/or spending hours outside. The downside? Waterproof gear will be slightly heavier, bulkier, and less breathable.

Don't Make This Mistake: Cotton

IS COTTON ROTTEN?

There's an old adage that "cotton kills." That refers to the fact that cotton holds on to moisture—so if you sweat in a cotton shirt, it will tend to stay wet and heavy and will lose its insulating abilities. In wet or cool weather, it's best to choose a synthetic fabric. However, there is one environment in which cotton can be beneficial: extreme, dry heat. In the desert, wearing a cotton shirt or cap that's been soaked in water will help keep you cool.

Gearing Up for Going Longer

Good news! You're all set for your first, short trail runs. But if you want to head into the mountains or forests for something more ambitious than a brief outing in a town park, you will need more gear. Here are our recommendations:

TRAIL RUNNING VEST

If you plan to run for longer than an hour, you'll want a trail running vest to carry water, energy snacks, and additional clothing. The good news is that sophisticated options abound in a variety of sizes.

Trail running vests feature either a water reservoir on your back or soft flasks—collapsible water bottles—that sit along the fronts of the shoulder straps. Try it before you buy it! Load it up and jog around the store. Look for a vest that fits your body: there should be minimal "bounce" as you run, with no irritating spots that might result in chafing. Water, your phone, and snacks should be easily accessible as you run.

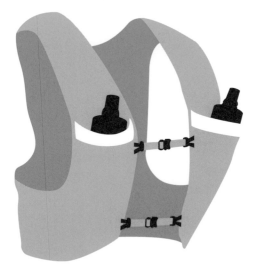

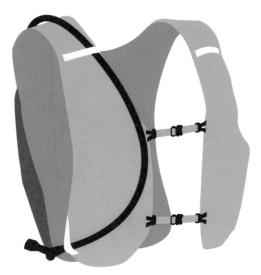

GPS WATCH

The more you trail run, the more you may want a good GPS-enabled watch to track your real-time pace and distance, keep tabs on your heart rate, analyze your training, and record the elevation profiles and routes of the trails you run.

These watches receive signals from Global Positioning System (GPS) satellites that runners use to track their location, movement data, and running performance.

Prices typically range from $300 to $600. If that's breaking your bank account, you can get started with a running or mapping app on your phone. A few of our favorites are Strava, FATMAP, CalTopo, Trail Run Project, OS Mapfinder, NeverAlone, Gaia GPS, and Google Earth.

WARNING

If you have to use a phone app during a trail run, you might find it hard to avoid the bad habit of checking text messages, emails, and voice-mails, just when you're trying to enjoy the freedom from technology that comes with getting out on the trails.

Here are key features to look for in a good GPS watch:

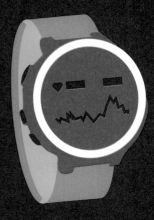

1. **HEART RATE MONITOR**
    Monitoring your heart rate before, during, and after a run can tell you a lot about your levels of fitness, fatigue, and recovery. More and more watches use wrist-based optical heart rate sensing technology. A word of caution: this technology can frequently be inaccurate, so only use optical monitors to get a rough sense of your heart rate. If you are serious about tracking heart rate, buy and wear a Bluetooth-connected chest strap that pairs with your watch.

2. **GPX TRACKS**
    Many GPS running watches include the ability to add and follow GPX and TPX routes. You can use those files for remote trails or off-trail running without having to open up Google Maps every five minutes when you've lost your bearings.

3. **SMARTPHONE INTEGRATION**
    If you don't like being tethered to your smartphone when you're out running trails but still want access to some of the apps and data on your phone, there are plenty of GPS watches that provide that kind of freedom.

4. **EASY INTEGRATION WITH ONLINE SERVICES**
    A number of online services allow you to track, save, and share data about your runs. Through these services, you can also connect with runners around the corner or across the globe, creating a new way of challenging yourself and making new trail running friends. The biggest of these companies is Strava, and each of the major watch brands offers its own service as well. Others include FATMAP, MapMyRun, Runkeeper, and Runtastic.

THE RISE OF STRAVA

Strava is the world's leading social fitness network. It is used primarily to track bike rides and runs via GPS. It is accessible via smartphones, watches, and numerous other mobile devices and is available in fourteen languages. Founded in 2009, Strava offers a free service and a monthly subscription plan with a wide range of features. Eight million activities are uploaded to Strava each day!

On Strava, your GPS-tracked trail runs can be broken down into smaller sections called segments. Segments designate specific features or portions of a route—such as a climb, a tricky stretch of trail, or a particularly fast and flat section. Each time you complete a segment, your time is recorded so you can compare it to previous efforts and those of your friends and other runners who have done the segment. You'll find that many of the trails you run contain preexisting segments, but you can also create your own Strava segments, too!

IT'S NOT ALL ABOUT THE GEAR

At the end of a great trail run, you'll remember the views, the wild places, the hard work that got you there, and the friends who joined in the fun. The gear? That just helps make it happen. Don't get pulled down the trail running industrial complex rabbit hole. It's about so much more than the gear.

ACCESSORIZE!

The longer you run, the more you'll need to take care of yourself in a variety of environmental conditions and at various levels of fatigue. Here's what we bring on a long trail run:

COMPRESSION LEG SLEEVES OR KNEE-HIGH COMPRESSION SOCKS

There is some evidence that compression clothing provides muscular support and improved blood flow to your calves, reducing fatigue on long runs.

ARM SLEEVES

Arm sleeves keep your arms comfortable when you're warming up or are running in variable weather conditions while wearing a T-shirt or tank top. They're also useful for sun protection. And on a hot day, try soaking them in water or adding a few ice cubes—that can really cool you off!

EARBUDS

Earbuds with Bluetooth connectivity allow for hassle-free listening while running. Many models also let in enough ambient noise that you can stay aware and in touch with your surroundings on the trail. Wireless, running-specific earbuds range from $60 to $200. There are also light-weight bone-conduction headphones that deliver music through your cheek-bones without obstructing your ears, eliminating many of the challenges of traditional headphones.

EMERGENCY BLANKET

A simple foil emergency blanket is an essential safety precaution if you're venturing out into the backcountry. Hypothermia can set in quickly if you twist an ankle and are unable to move. Emergency blankets are cheap, lightweight insurance.

ANTI-CHAFING LUBRICANT

These rub-on sticks can be a lifesaver if your skin tends to chafe at friction-prone spots. Some come in compact tubes, so you can bring them on your run and apply as needed.

GLOVES

You're going to want your fingers to work, no matter the temp. If you think it's likely to get chilly, toss in a pair of non-cotton, lightweight gloves. They weigh next to nothing and will keep you from opening zippers with your teeth.

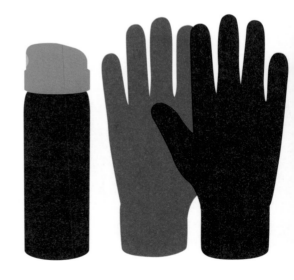

HEADLAMP

A comfortably fitting, bright head-lamp can help you navigate the woods during dawn, dusk, or nighttime runs. Eco tip: look for one with a recharge-able battery.

INSTANT WARMERS

Manufactured under various names, these small, single-use chemical heaters work wonders on chilly fingers and toes.

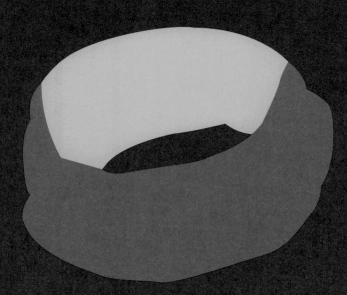

NECK GAITER

Sometimes referred to by the brand name Buff, this tube of lightweight nylon or merino wool fabric is won-derfully versatile as a hat, ear/neck/wrist/hand warmer, face mask, hair tie, or improvised running belt. It can even be used for first aid, as a sling or bandage! Neck gaiters are a staple in many trail runners' gear closets.

PAPER MAP

For anything more than a short run in a park, it's important to bring a paper map—not just the one on your phone. (Remember Murphy's Law? When you most need it, the battery on your phone will die!) It should cover not just the area you're running, but also the region around your run, in case you get lost.

POLES

To help save your leg muscles and give you better balance on long runs on steep terrain, look for a pair of ultralight, collapsible, foldable trail running–specific poles, such as Black Diamond's Distance Carbon Z poles. Refer to size charts to ensure the correct length.

RUNNING GAITERS

Gaiters wrap around your ankles and prevent debris from getting into your shoes. They're most helpful on dusty or sandy desert trails, or exceptionally muddy ground.

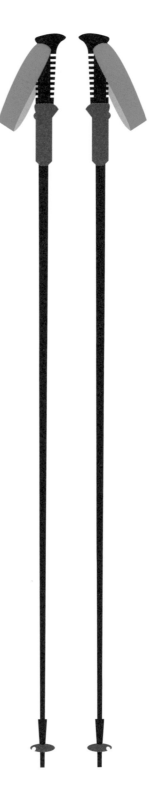

TRACTION DEVICES

If you might be running on icy or snowy terrain, traction devices are prudent. These lightweight sets of metal spikes or coils attach to the soles of your running shoes to offer more purchase on ice.

WATER PURIFICATION

If you're planning a long run in a remote setting, you'll want to carry a lightweight water-treatment system so that you can drink safely from mountain streams. Research the many available options—everything from iodine tablets to filter bottles to straws—and go with what will work best for you.

SUNGLASSES

When shopping for sunglasses, look for lightweight models designed for running that won't bounce around as you run. Sunglasses that transition from light to dark are ideal if you're going to be in a variety of settings, from alpine areas to snowfields to forests.

TAKE SOME TUNES. OR NOT?

Listening to music or podcasts when trail running can be controversial. Listening to your surroundings helps keep you tuned in to your environment, so you can hear everything from snakes to speedier trail runners sneaking up on you from behind. It also lets you communicate more easily with other trail users when one of you wants to pass the other. And listening to the sound of your feet on the trail, and the birds keeping you company, will keep you more "present" on your run, reducing some of that stress you've built up from your hours in the office.

However, if you want to run with tunes, we're not going to stop you. Consider running with just one earbud in, though, or choosing non-noise-cancelling earbuds and keeping the volume low enough that you can still communicate with other trail users. To get you rocking down the trail, we've crowdsourced a few playlists for you and shared a few of our favorite podcasts! Use the QR code to immediately access the list on Spotify.

WARM UP MIX

HIGH INTENSITY MIX

COOL DOWN MIX

Get the tunes! Just open your Spotify app, go to the search section, and click on the camera symbol.

TRAIL RUNNING PODCASTS

Billy Yang Podcast
DNF Podcast
Fastest Known Podcast
Kicksology Podcast
Science of Ultra
Talk Ultra

The Morning Shakeout
The Rich Roll Podcast
Trail Runner Nation
Trail Running Women
Ultrarunnerpodcast

TEST IT OUT!

Find a trail festival, race, or event with brand ambassadors doing demos, and try out products, vests, and a cornucopia of other trail running gear. By testing gear, you'll be better able to understand the nuanced differences—and you'll find the items that are exactly right for you!

CHAPTER 4

FUEL FOR THE FIRE

When you are running on a trail, trillions of your cells act as little power centers. Each of those cells is powered by the food and liquid you put into your body. Imagine a cabin in the woods on a cold winter day with a big woodstove inside. Add plenty of dry hardwood, and the fire will burn hot for a long time. But if soggy sticks are all you have the cabin's never going to get warm. It's the same with your body. Skimp on fuel or put bad raw materials into your power plant, and you'll bonk—deplete your muscles' carbohydrate stores and hit a wall—on your next run.

Your need for high-quality fuel doesn't stop when you get off the trails, either. Your body is constantly repairing itself and adapting to the stress of exercise—both of which require fuel and hydration, too. Inadequate fueling can slow your progress and increase your risk of getting injured.

There's good news here for all of us. Unlike factors like genetics, fueling and hydration are entirely under our control. By considering what you eat and drink (this means you, Big Mac and Pop-Tarts!), you can be healthier, happier, and speedier.

Hydration

The first step in taking control of your fueling and hydration is to make sure you have adequate fluids. Proper hydration lets your body clear waste products and is essential for nearly every bodily function, including running.

GENERAL HYDRATION TIPS—FOR ON AND OFF THE TRAIL

1. After you wake up, drink a glass of water. While you were dreaming, your body was still humming along performing basic tasks, all of which use a bit of water. A quick glass of water will prevent you from starting the day with your "low on fluids" light on.

2. Throughout the day, stay hydrated—as feels natural to you. Experts have differing views here, so we suggest looking at what the pros do. Most elite runners carry a water bottle around with them each day. Grabbing a few sips of water here and there is a simple thing to do—it won't hurt, and it'll keep the water flowing into your body.

3. Your body absorbs water more readily if there are some electrolytes mixed in. So consider adding a pinch of salt or an electrolyte tab to that bottle you're now carrying around with you.

4. While electrolytes are good, drinking sugary water is not. Unfortunately, many sports drinks contain added sugar. Fruit juice contains plenty of natural sugars, too. Too many of these liquid calories have been linked to obesity and Type 2 diabetes. So watch what's in your water!

5. When it's time to crash for the day, make sure you aren't going to bed dehydrated. If you find yourself parched when you wake up, you might want to experiment with a small glass of water before bed. (Waking up to pee all night long? You're overdoing it!)

BEFORE YOU LACE UP

Being well hydrated at the start of runs ensures that your body will produce energy as efficiently as possible, so start with your tank full! A general guideline is to try to drink 12 to 16 ounces (0.35 L to 0.5 L) of fluids in the 60 to 75 minutes before your run. Experiment with what works for you—different bodies have different needs!

DURING YOUR RUN

Just out for an hour? There's no need to be chained to your water bottle. If you start the run hydrated and are going for less than 60 minutes, you shouldn't need to rehydrate until you're done.

On runs longer than 60 minutes, the amount of hydration needed depends upon how much water you're losing through sweating, which is also known as your sweat rate. Everybody is different, and the variation in rates can be astounding. In general, smaller athletes require less fluid, and bigger athletes require more. But there are some 100-pound runners who sweat like broken fire hydrants and some 250-pound runners who just barely glisten. In addition, temperature and dew point play a big role in how much you sweat. On hot, humid days, you'll need more no matter your sweat rate.

Generally speaking, however, most trail runners require 12 to 24 ounces (0.35 L to 0.7 L) of fluid per hour, depending on sweat rate and weather. And having some extra calories in your fluids can aid absorption and stave off bonking. Sports drinks and mixes with electrolytes are better than plain water—just watch for those added sugars!

Beyond two hours, be sure to hydrate properly. Plan your runs around water sources, invest in a water filter or tablets, or stash bottles along your run. While it's possible to run without food, running without water is a recipe for disaster.

AND WHEN YOU'RE DONE

After you finish running, there are few more pleasant experiences than a tall glass of cold water. So indulge, you earned it! In general, you should rehydrate whatever sweat loss you failed to keep up with during exercise. If you're feeling adventurous, you can mix water and juice, or even add a scoop of protein powder.

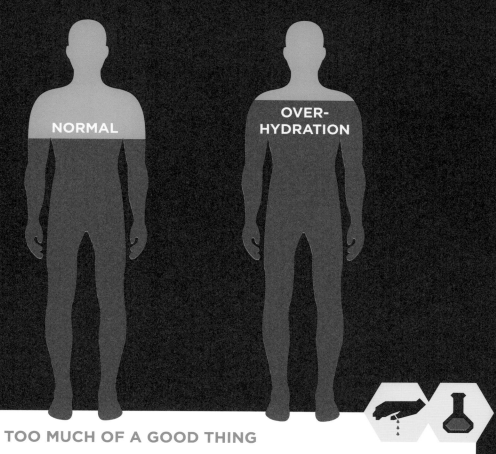

NORMAL

OVER-HYDRATION

TOO MUCH OF A GOOD THING

Hydration is essential, but as with anything, it's possible to have too much of a good thing, too. Avoid overhydration, which can cause kidney damage and even death. Overhydration, or hyponatremia, is a major risk if you aren't listening to your body and guzzle massive amounts of fluids.

CALCULATE YOUR SWEAT RATE

Where do you fall on the fire-hydrant-to-camel spectrum? Well, your partner can tell you! But for a more precise and less adjective-filled result, try this method before a 60-to-90-minute run:

1. Hydrate normally pre-run and pee before heading out the door.

2. Right before you hit the trails, weigh yourself.

3. Run normally, preferably at the intensities you are aiming to quantify. For example, if you want to know your sweat rate for a race, run at race pace.

4. No peeing allowed while you run. (This will be especially difficult if you have an overactive bladder. Stay strong!)

5. After running, towel dry the sweat on your skin and hair, then hop on the scale again.

6. Multiply the pounds lost by 16 ounces (0.5 L) to get a general approximation of your sweat rate.

When it comes time to run, keep that number in mind. Of course, it will vary based on the weather, so repeat this exercise in different conditions. And when you're out there running, remember that it's fine to be a bit slow on replacing fluids, but if you fall too far behind, your trail running will suffer.

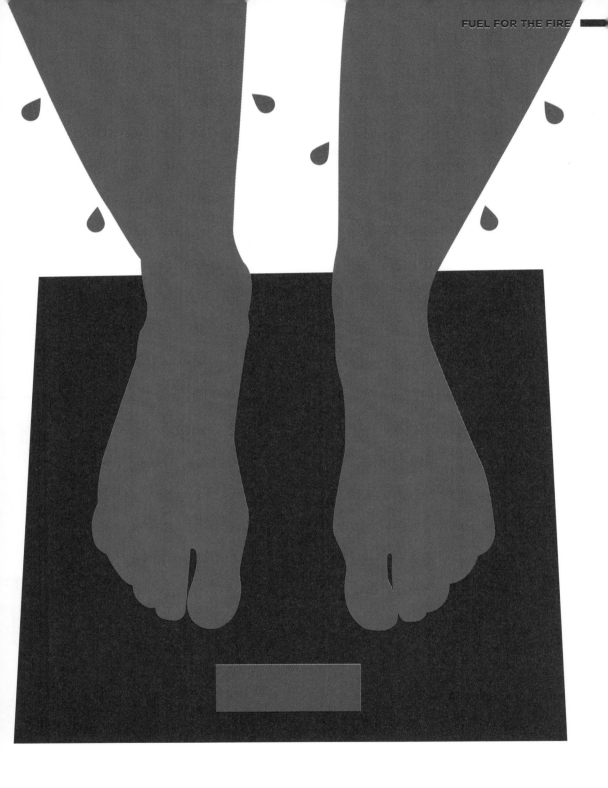

Fueling 101

What you eat is venturing dangerously close to who you vote for or where you pray. In other words, diet has a way of moving from science-based practices to something more akin to a belief system. So this primer is not designed to say what you should do, but to provide a general template to work from.

BURN RATE

This varies a lot, so we won't break it down here, but running 1 mile (1.6 km) can burn up to 100 calories, with variation for age, gender, weight, and running experience. So generally, if you run a lot, you need to eat a lot.

Failing to fuel enough can work in the short term for some people who need to lose weight. But long-term negative energy availability while training can lead to overuse injuries, reduced libido, and countless other maladies that make running (and life) far less enjoyable. So the stakes are high when it comes to running-related fueling.

At the threshold level, make sure you are getting enough calories for your goals. That is step number one—avoid thinking that less is more and skinny is fast. Instead, reframe it in this way: "Strong is fast." To be strong, you must fuel.

WHAT'S YOUR BMR?

Your body has a basal metabolic rate (BMR), which is the baseline number of calories it takes to maintain your body's functions without going into energy debt. Going below your BMR is good if you are trying to lose weight, but it can also lead to running-related injuries and overtraining syndrome due to lack of fuel to repair your body.

BMR varies from person to person. BMR is higher for men who have a higher body mass index (BMI) and lower for women with lower BMIs. For example, the BMR for a 5'2", 25-year-old sedentary woman weighing 110 pounds is 1200 calories per day. Meanwhile, a 6'5", 250-pound man of the same age has a BMR of 2070 daily calories. Want to know your BMR? There are several easy-to-use calculators online.

BUT WHAT TO EAT?

The food you eat is made up of three key macronutrients—fats, proteins, and carbohydrates. Each of them plays a role in moving you forward on the trail.

FATS

Fat is essential for fueling your trail run. Some fats are better than others, though. The general principle is that "good" fat is the healthiest part of a well-rounded diet. When you can, choose foods like nuts and avocados over the fats in red meat and processed snack foods. The debate isn't over, though, and some proponents of high-fat diets argue that traditional "bad fats" like bacon are actually healthy at low levels.

Sources of healthy fat include nuts and nut butters, fish such as salmon and trout, and tofu.

Reserve special, fatty treats, such as ice cream, more than a pat of butter, and red meat, for periods when you've been training hard. And even then, eat them in moderation.

PROTEINS

Next on our list are the proteins and amino acids that are essential for muscle and cell repair. There are estimates for grams you need per kilogram of body weight, but they vary widely. Instead of doing more math, here's our advice: have a protein of some type at every meal.

Great sources of protein include beans, peas, lentils, white fish, and full-fat cottage cheese. Reserve protein sources such as sausage and other processed meats, as well as processed protein bars with added sugar, for special occasions.

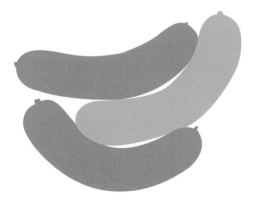

CARBS

Carbohydrates are essential for energy during exercise, and they break down into two categories: simple and complex. Simple carbs digest easily and rapidly, giving a quick hit of energy—perfect for immediately before, during, or after your trail runs. Complex carbs contain more fiber and nutrients, so they take more time for your body to process, but generally provide more nutritional benefits. They are best consumed during your meals outside of workouts. Because carbs are necessary to keep your body efficient during hard trail runs, a good rule is to not skimp on simple carbs before, during, or immediately after runs, and to enjoy complex carbs in moderation the rest of the time. Note that some foods such as fiber-rich fruits (think apples, bananas, or berries) contain both simple and complex carbs.

Some sources of simple carbs include fresh or dried fruit, white bread, bagels, white rice, many types of pasta, and energy gels and chews. Some sources of complex carbs include vegetables, fruit, whole wheat bread, brown rice, sweet potatoes, oats, and beans.

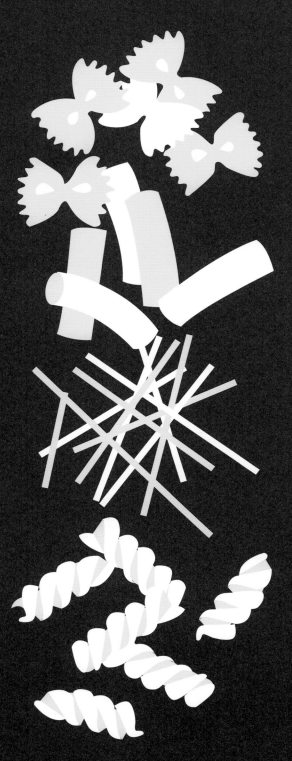

PRO-LEVEL SNACKING

Among top runners, there are foods that you'll see again and again in their fridges and in their Instagram posts. Here are the top five.

TOP FIVE SNACKS FOR TRAIL RUNNERS

1. **FULL-FAT YOGURT**
   Full-fat yogurt provides a nearly ideal macronutrient profile when mixed with a dollop of honey. It has protein plus probiotics, which could improve gut health and prevent mid-run stops in the bushes.

2. **NUTS AND NUT BUTTERS**
   There is almost no diet that says nuts are bad, which is remarkable because nearly every food is controversial if you know the right person to ask. Countless runners practically live on almond butter.

3. **BEEF JERKY**
   Jerky is a great source of protein. Trail runners love it so much that jerky sponsorships are not uncommon among pro runners.

4. **BANANAS**
   US trail runner Zach Miller is lovingly called "Banana Boy" by some of his closest friends. Why? He has been known to eat almost a dozen a day on occasion.

5. **EGGS**
   Eggs with yolks are a wonderful source of many essential nutrients, and an omelet is a great option for post-long-run brunch.

VITAMINS AND MINERALS THAT MATTER

Even today, the question of whether to supplement your diet with vitamins is contentious. (Bored? Google "Should I take vitamins?" and check out the passionate answers!) We're not going to take a side, but we will share information about some supplemental vitamins and minerals that trail runners commonly use. These include:

VITAMIN D

Vitamin D is essential for bone health and a strong cardiovascular system, and it supports your immune system—all things central to being a healthy trail runner. Your body makes its own vitamin D when your skin is exposed to sunlight, but if you're not seeing the sun enough, consider an additional 1000 to 5000 IU per day, at the direction of a doctor.

IRON

Iron is essential for making healthy red blood cells, and iron deficiencies can hurt performance, making runners feel like trail zombies. Most top female runners take an iron supplement of between 18 mg and 65 mg. But male runners should get a blood test before taking an iron supplement, since too much iron can be harmful. Strange but true: running breaks down iron through something called "foot strike hemolysis," where cells are damaged during each footfall.

MULTIVITAMIN

While a multivitamin may be unnecessary if you have all of your diet boxes checked, it is sometimes difficult to get everything you need if you are frequently on the go, trying to eat at airport terminals before your next flight. Consider a multivitamin if this describes you!

A Peek Inside the Furnace

Ready for the nitty-gritty of fueling? Great! Here's the secret to the furnace within each of us.

Most of your energy is stored and used in one of two ways. Your glycogen stores— basically, stored carbohy- drates—are topped off from meals many hours before your run, and they can fuel high- intensity exercise for 90 to 120 minutes. The second form of energy is your fat stores—the jiggle when you wiggle. Your fat stores can burn nearly indefinitely, though at a lower intensity than glycogen.

Glycogen burns hot, so you'll be calling on it when your training is more in- tense. Fat stores burn long and strong, so lower-intensity exercise uses fat. In practice, most trail running mixes those two energy sources. That is why most runners *could* go three hours without keeling over, although they may have to slow down.

BEFORE YOUR RUN

Your pre-run meal should be focused on topping off your glycogen stores and optimizing your blood sugar for the activity ahead. For most runners, something small with about 200 to 300 calories does the trick, like an energy bar or a banana and peanut butter. It's best consumed a couple of hours before the run.

Some trail runners, however, will get upset stomachs if they try to eat hours before running. Others can eat a full meal moments before hitting the trails. Figure out where you fall on the spectrum. What matters most is that you've been eating well in the days before your run.

DURING YOUR RUN

During runs, your body burns through both glycogen and fat. For intense runs less than 90 minutes, you don't need to refuel. And for lower-intensity events under two to three hours, you don't need anything either, since your body will likely be burning your fat stores.

However, once your more intense workout ticks past about 90 minutes, or your lower-intensity run extends for more than a few hours, you'll need to refuel. (Unless you are a fat-adapted runner, that is. See the sidebar on page 77.) Typically, running burns anywhere from 500 to 1000 calories an hour. Meanwhile, our stomachs can only tolerate about 300 calories per hour during exercise. No matter what, you will develop a calorie deficit. The key is to prevent that deficit from becoming too big and causing a bonk, where your engine room runs out of fuel and forward motion just about grinds to a stop.

You can get those 300 calories per hour from whatever sources you tolerate. Typically, energy gels are the most reliable option. A gel eaten after 60 minutes and then every 30 minutes thereafter, supplemented by a sports drink, can work wonders for energy levels and performance. Other options are energy bars, or even more outside-the-box treats like peanut butter and jelly sandwiches. But if you train your stomach over time, it usually has a remarkable ability to handle almost anything. Trail runner Clare Gallagher famously won the 2016 Leadville 100 in the second-fastest women's time ever while fueling with . . . wait for it . . . frosting and candy! Clare showed us all that the key is to minimize the calorie deficit, rather than to consume the perfect foods every single moment.

AFTER YOUR RUN

As a general rule, focus first on rehydration after you finish your run. Then, let yourself be guided by hunger, with the qualification that you should be sure to get well-rounded foods with carbs, protein, and fat in your body within an hour or two of running, if possible.

Have fun with post-run foods, and don't be afraid of giving yourself a reward. Positive psychology works, and it's really fun to treat yourself like a puppy on occasion!

FAT ADAPTATION AND FASTED RUNNING

The body is astonishingly adaptable, and that is especially evident in how it can be trained to utilize fat. Over time, with specific dietary choices, an athlete can burn more fat at higher levels of exertion, theoretically leading to more efficiency on the trails.

A few general principles can help every trail runner:

1. **EAT A HIGH-FAT DIET**
   Diets higher in good fats relative to carbohydrates and proteins make it easier to burn fat while running.

2. **DO SOME RUNS AFTER A BIT OF FASTING**
   Periodically, head out on a morning run prior to consuming any calories after waking up. This will teach your body to access fat stores sooner.

3. **CONSUME FEWER CALORIES ON OCCASION**
   This method, like fasting and running, teaches your body to access fat stores more easily. Experiment with this on one of your long, slow run days.

Golden Rules to Fuel By

Fueling and hydration are big parts of our lives that are dramatically complicated by misinformation, twisted social norms that encourage unhealthy eating, and deceptive marketing. As a result, diet and body image can easily get mixed up with feelings of self-worth. To stay happy and healthy while fueling up, follow these simple guidelines:

1. DON'T WAKE UP HUNGRY
If you find yourself waking up with an almost uncontrollable urge to eat, you are underfueling. Because underfueling can cause health issues for runners, it's essential to heed signals that you need to head to the kitchen.

2. AVOID OVERTRAINING—IT'S INSIDIOUS
Overtraining syndrome takes many forms, from hormone deficiencies to overuse injuries, and it happens to runners of all abilities. Some physiologists believe that overtraining is due in part to inadequate fueling. So be sure you're taking on plenty of calories when you're trail running hard.

3. DO EVERYTHING IN MODERATION
By our nature, we runners can be a bit obsessive-compulsive. To counteract that tendency, practice the old axiom: everything in moderation—including moderation! Eat well, and every now and then splurge on that large, quadruple-cheese pizza and the pint of gelato after. Chances are, you've more than earned it.

4. TOSS THE SCALE OUT THE WINDOW
Or at least put it into a dark corner of your closet. For many trail runners, moving away from obsessing about weight can be the first step toward a healthier relationship with food. Viewing your body only in terms of quantified inputs and outputs will take the soul away from day-to-day life and may lead to eating disorders and body dysmorphia.

5. DON'T OVERTHINK IT
It's a good idea to set yourself some rules, like eating a lot of healthy fat and not bingeing on a huge bag of Doritos every night. But once that's done, focus on what your body is telling you, rather than what the media, society, and fad diet "experts" are telling you. Viewing your diet through the lens of general goals rather than strict rules is liberating. And it will ultimately lead to better health outcomes.

YOU ARE WHAT YOU EAT

The next time you are running down a trail at full speed, think about what your body is going through. Feel your quads absorbing the impact, your feet pushing off the ground, and your muscles contracting at full strength. Then think of the saying "You are what you eat."

In that moment, what sort of food do you want to have powering you? Certainly not a glazed jelly donut. But you also don't want it to be a leaf of lettuce. Instead, you want it to be a three-egg omelet with mushrooms and spinach, or whole grain avocado toast with a side of sweet potato fries. In other words, when the going gets tough, you want to be fueled by food that is built to go the distance.

Food is strength, and strength means you'll get to go both fast and long on the trails. Make fueling and hydration choices that make you strong, and you'll be happily hammering out miles on the trails for decades to come.

TAKE IT TO THE NEXT LEVEL

Get a grip on the ingredients. Many of today's energy bars and gels are filled with chemicals only a PhD scientist would recognize— Frankenfoods that are created in a lab, with extra sugar added, too. To keep it healthy, go DIY and make your own bars and gels at home. You can find plenty of recipes online, or grab a copy of the book *Feed Zone Portables*. (Psst: You'll save enough cash to buy those new trail running shoes you've been coveting, too!)

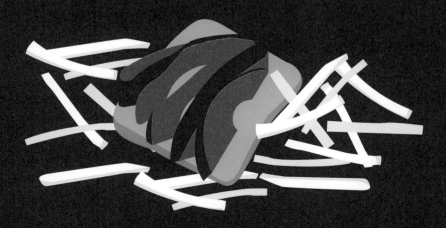

CHAPTER 5

GETTING FIT FOR THE TRAILS

The first time you go for a trail run, even if you're a seasoned road runner with a high level of fitness, you might find it to be more challenging than you expected. The hills, rugged terrain, and all of the twisting trails can seem downright relentless, making you feel:

1. light-headed, dead-legged, and gasping for air;
2. discouraged, distraught, and dejected;
3. curious as to why you left the pavement in the first place; and/or
4. confused about why a sport that is so popular can be so damned hard.

The good news is that those feelings and thoughts are temporary. (We promise!) Trail running will get easier as you gain trail running–specific fitness. For example, during a typical run on roads, your heart rate and effort increase gradually from start to finish. In trail running, however, your heart rate can go a little haywire. That's because one of the biggest differences in trail running—especially on hilly or mountainous terrain—is that your heart rate can spike early during your run and never recover to those lower levels. For that reason, you need a different kind of fitness to be able to run efficiently and effectively without becoming overcome by fatigue or weariness.

Building trail running fitness takes time. The best way to get there is by following a consistent training program. Training to become a better trail runner should include several specific areas of focus, including aerobic development, functional strength, agility, speed, and terrain-specific development. This chapter breaks down each of those categories.

Aerobic Development

The foundation of trail running is aerobic development, which comes from consistent, slow to moderate "easy" miles. Aerobic development is a process by which your body becomes more efficient at processing oxygen and creating energy. Aerobic running is lower intensity, meaning your muscles have enough oxygen to do their work, relying only on aerobic metabolism to make the energy they need. Primarily, aerobic running burns fat, rather than carbohydrates, allowing the body to become more efficient with this readily available fuel source.

SIGNS THAT YOU'RE PROBABLY RUNNING AT AN AEROBIC PACE

- You're not on super-steep terrain. Aerobic trail running is most often done on easy to moderate terrain without a lot of climbing.

- You can chat with your running buddies without secretly fearing you might be having a heart attack. Talking with your pals is one of the best aspects of trail running. If you find yourself gasping for breath and can't talk in more than four-word sentences, slow down a bit and enjoy the journey, knowing that you're building your strength as you chitchat.

- Your pulse isn't pounding so strongly that you can feel it all over your body.

LACTATE THRESHOLD TESTING

You can use a bit of technology to understand your running speed at lactate threshold (RSLT), one of the best indicators of your running fitness and the most reliable predictor of endurance performance. RSLT is the running speed or heart rate at which lactate—an intermediate product of aerobic metabolism in the muscles—begins to accumulate rapidly in the bloodstream. Your lactate threshold (LT) is a point during all-out exercise at which lactate builds in the bloodstream faster than the body can remove it and therefore forces the body to ease up to avoid complete muscular fatigue.

Having a higher lactate threshold means an athlete can continue at a high-intensity effort with a longer time to exhaustion. The average person reaches their lactate threshold at 60 percent of their VO2 max—a measurement of maximum exertion. A fit recreational trail runner reaches their LT at 65–80 percent of their VO2 max, while an elite trail runner hits their LT at 85–95 percent of their VO2 max.

In addition to being useful as a measure of running fitness, lactate threshold can also help you establish individual target intensity zones to guide your training. Doing so requires that you know the running pace and/or heart rate that corresponds to your LT.

HOW TO DETERMINE RSLT

Put yourself through a 30-minute RSLT time trial, that's how!

1. Begin with several minutes of easy jogging to warm up.

2. When you're ready, start tracking time, distance, and pace on your watch or smartphone app. Run for 30 minutes at the fastest pace you can sustain.

3. Be careful to avoid the common mistake of starting too fast and then slowing down toward the end of the time trial due to fatigue, which will produce an inaccurate result.

4. When you get to 10 minutes, note your heart rate.

5. At 30 minutes, stop and note your heart rate again.

6. Calculate the sum of those two heart rates and divide by two. That's your lactate threshold heart rate! While your result might fall in a range of 150–180 beats per minute, for most active people, lactate threshold is about 20 beats per minute above their steady aerobic threshold. Generally speaking, younger athletes will have higher lactate threshold heart rates than older athletes.

SO WHY GO AEROBIC?

Here are some benefits of aerobic running:

- It improves how efficiently your body pumps blood and energizes working muscles, making you faster no matter your effort.

- It builds strength in muscles, tendons, and bones. That strength is essential for efficient trail running and the prevention of overuse injuries.

- It's fun and sustainable. Since it shouldn't ever hurt, aerobic training makes it easier to keep to your training goals.

IT'S ALL IN THE NUMBERS

One big difference between trail running and road running is how a long run is measured. Road runners who are training for a 10 km race or a marathon will typically talk about their training in terms of distance, but trail runners mostly track their training in the amount of time they spend on their feet.

Why the difference? Simple. The variability of trail terrain can make distance an inconsistent measure. For example, a 10 km or 6-mile run on a road or flat path will take most runners 40 to 60 minutes, but that same distance could take two hours or longer on hilly or mountainous trails.

10 KM

2 HOURS

10 KM

40–60 MINUTES

HOW LONG SHOULD A LONG RUN BE, ANYWAY?

The basis of every distance trail running training program is a weekly long run. But the duration of that long run will vary greatly depending on your experience and goals. So you might hear fellow trail runners talking about running crazy distances or long hours. Should you be doing the same as them? Probably not.

New trail runners might consider a 60-minute run to be long, while experienced ultra-distance trail runners might run for 6 to 8 hours for their long run. Here are a few guidelines to figure out what's right for you.

- If you're just starting trail running and have 3 to 5 hours a week available, your once-a-week long run should be no longer than about 90 minutes.

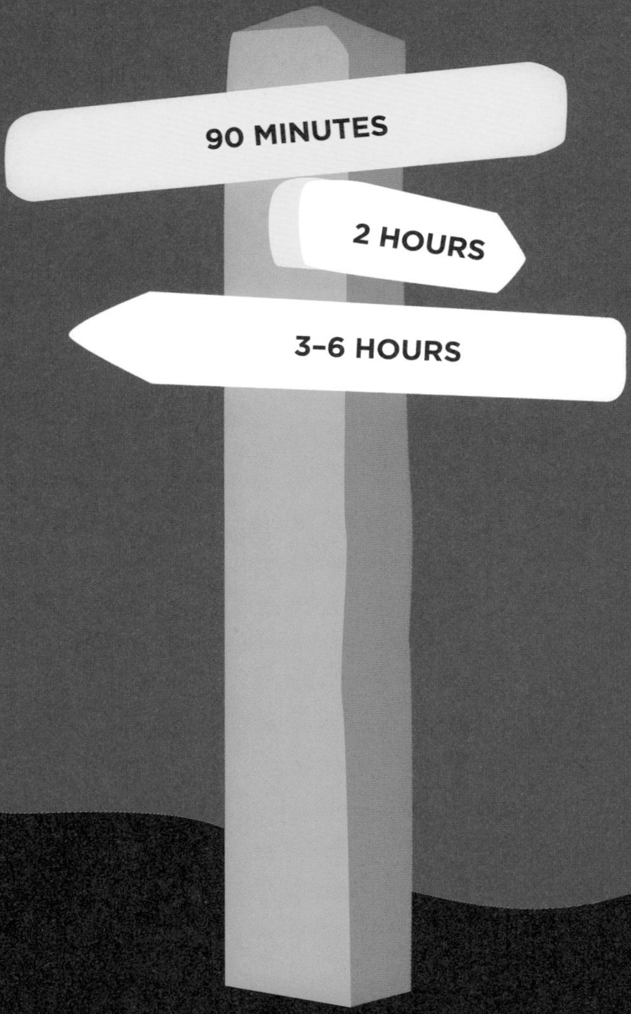

90 MINUTES

2 HOURS

3-6 HOURS

- If you're an intermediate runner who does 6 to 10 hours of running per week, your long run should max out at 2 hours.

- For those running 10 hours or more per week, your long run might range from 3 to 6 hours.

HAVE FUN, BUILD COMMUNITY

Weekly long runs can sometimes feel like a chore. If that happens, shake it up and increase the fun factor and sense of community of your run by . . .

- Planning it a few days in advance with friends, coworkers, and running pals. Not only will this keep you accountable, but the shared joy, mutual enthusiasm, and engaging conversation will take away any burden created by the rigors of trail running.

- Selecting a unique, scenic trail or remote trail. Striking out for new territory can add zest to your experience.

- Planning to share a post-run meal at a favorite restaurant. Nothing eases the struggle of those final miles like banter about whether you'll be ordering the triple-decker jumbo cheeseburger or the two-pound monster burrito featuring the Trinidad scorpion hot pepper.

- Making it a weekly event. This might just be the start of your own, informal trail running club! Invite others, seek out new trails each week, pick new restaurants and pubs, and even train for trail races together.

Get Stronger, Go Longer

When you start trail running, you might be overwhelmed by how long and far some of your running buddies can go. Or you might get discouraged and think training for a 50 km (31-mile) or 50-mile (80 km) race is absurd. But you also might start having moments of inspiration where you'll crave running longer for a variety of reasons—to explore more remote trails, see more sights, and set bigger race goals.

The good news is that you can get there. But it takes time. Once you've built an aerobic base, you can start adding more definition to your trail running fitness by gradually improving your strength and endurance. Both are based on increasing your muscular strength, improving your athleticism, and stretching your aerobic capacity.

Strength isn't about developing big muscles and getting stronger; it's about developing running-specifc musculature to allow you to more effectively and efficiently move over a trail. While that might mean increasing the strength of your hamstrings and calf muscles, in most cases it means developing the micro-muscles in your feet, lower legs, and core to make you more agile, nimble, powerful, and stable while running on uneven surfaces.

Endurance, on the other hand, is the ability to run longer. But it's more than just slogging through a lot of hours on the trail. It's the ability to run better for an extended time without having your performance and efficiency decline from muscular fatigue and general weariness.

So how do you build strength and endurance?

One great way is by starting to run faster. Once you are comfortable with your long run and your base level of fitness, it's time to work on raising your aerobic threshold, so you can run faster while still powering yourself with aerobic metabolism. Raising your aerobic threshold involves running at a slightly more intense pace than pure aerobic running. A couple of times each week, replace your normal easy run with a moderately hard 20-to-30-minute "tempo" run, where you can still talk, but only in short, choppy sentences.

Aerobic threshold running over variable terrain builds both resilience and endurance, since your body is adapting to uphills and downhills at a moderate pace. Design these runs so that they involve every type of terrain you enjoy—especially steep ups and downs, once you are comfortable running them. If you are newer to trail running, have patience—your musculoskeletal system will adapt over the course of a few months.

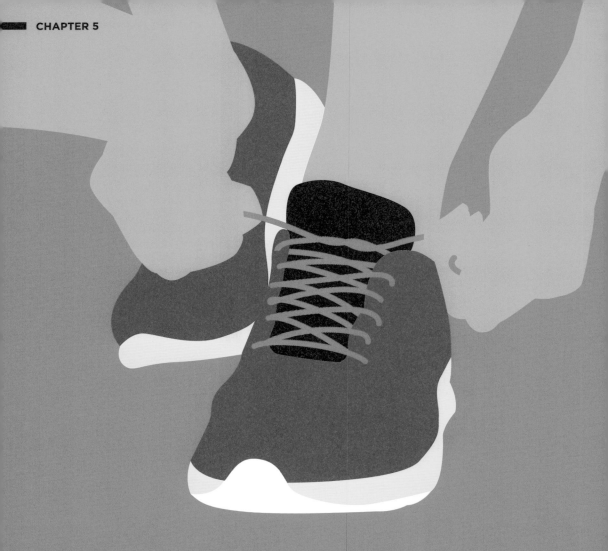

A CORE CURRICULUM

Trail running is a simple sport. It's as easy as lacing up your shoes and putting one foot in front of the other. The two simplest ways of improving as a trail runner are by running trails more and working on your core strength.

Here's why core strength matters. Improving the strength in your abs, lower back, hips, and upper body will improve your balance and stability out on the trails. It will also allow more muscle groups to share the workload. Does that mean you have to hit the gym and pump it up like Arnold Schwarzenegger? Not at all. But if you do a simple core strength program a couple of times per week, you'll go a long way toward prepping your body for years of healthy trail running. There are dozens of strength maintenance programs online, but generally your program should include maintaining and building your core—your hips, glutes, abs, lower back—so you can properly support your body and remain stable out on the trails. Focus on quality, not quantity, keeping good form and activating a lot of muscle groups. You can easily develop your own 10-minute routine by combining various sets of sit-ups, push-ups, planks, side planks, leg raises, and single-leg squats. Doing that just two to three times a week is all you need!

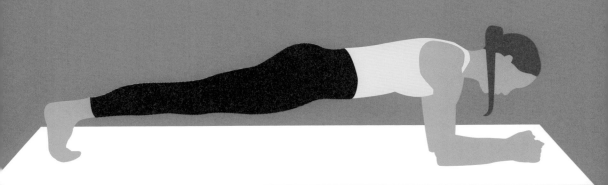

Get Faster

One of the last key pieces to building your trail running fitness is developing speed. We're not talking about world-class-sprinter-level quickness but instead about the ability to sustain faster paces for longer periods of time. That might mean running a fast 5 km trail race or sustaining a relatively fast pace—for you—for a half or full marathon distance on trails.

Workouts come in all shapes and sizes, but at their core they all involve sustaining moderate to hard efforts. This improves running economy (that is, your efficiency) and aerobic fitness, with the added benefit of boosting you into higher levels of training. This, in turn, allows your body to push harder, faster, and longer—as long as you don't get injured from the increased demands on your musculoskeletal system or burnt out from the increased mental energy it takes to make it hurt a little bit.

Running intervals—or short, faster, and harder periods broken up with longer periods of slower running—is one great way to pick up your pace. Here's how to get started.

FOR YOUR
FIRST WEEK OR TWO . . .

Start with a run that includes short and simple intervals of about 20 to 30 seconds each in which you are running faster and harder. Like the quick strides discussed in Chapter 2, shorter intervals allow you to focus on proper running mechanics. Do your best to stay smooth and effortless.

. . . THEN FOR
A COUPLE OF MORE WEEKS . . .

Progress it to ten 1-minute intervals at a moderately hard, fast (but not all-out) pace with 1 minute of easy running in between. You can do these intervals on any type of terrain. If you want to get faster, run them on flat or rolling trails; if you want to get stronger, run them on uphills and downhills. After your first week increase the number of intervals, then lengthen them to 2 minutes the next week, and 3 minutes the week after that.

. . . AND KEEP THIS UP!

As your body adapts, you can add longer, lower-intensity intervals, like six 5-minute intervals at a moderately hard pace, with 3 minutes' recovery, then three 10-minute intervals with a 5-minute recovery, or even longer tempos between 20 minutes and an hour in length. If you want to add a second workout to the week, you can incorporate these workouts into your long run as well. It's okay if your total weekly running volume drops slightly, but don't let it drop too much. While workouts are great for short-term breakthroughs, long-term success is founded on sustained training volume.

RUN DRILLS AND STRIDES

One of the keys to getting faster as a runner is to improve stride efficiency, cadence, and speed through focusing on your form and strength. Repetitive drills that exaggerate an aspect of good running form are especially important for running on trails, because every single step you take is unique.

The subtle strength and muscle memory gained from doing drills several times per week will help boost neuromuscular reaction time, increase stride cadence, and improve stability on variable terrain, while also reducing your chance of getting injured. What kinds of drills are we talking about? High knees, butt kicks, bounding, grapevines or Carioca (a sideways-moving drill that entails the crisscrossing of the legs), single-leg squats or step-ups, and various forms of skipping will all help make you a better and healthier trail runner.

4%–8%

RUN LIKE THE WIND

Adding a series of short wind sprints is a good way to improve strength, durability, running economy, and speed. Wind sprints are different from running intervals on a track or flat trail, because they require more explosive power yet result in less impact on your body.

As your introduction to faster running, start with hill strides, which have less pounding on your muscles and joints. Find a very gradual hill between 4 and 8 percent gradient (really, anything between flat and the steepest road you've driven), and after a 15-minute warm-up—or after a 45-minute easy run—run 20 to 30 seconds moderately hard up the hill. While you are running, focus on smooth and sustainable form—in other words, use long-distance running form, not sprinting form. Jog down easily for recovery, and repeat four to eight times, two or three times per week.

7 TRAINING DON'TS

With the dozens of possible workouts you can do on all sorts of trails, sometimes things can go a bit off the rails. Here are some of the most common ways training can go wrong. Keep them in mind as you build your trail running strength, endurance, and speed.

1. Don't make it up as you go along. Follow a training plan. Running too much or too little will leave you fatigued if you have a big race coming up.

2. Don't do a hard workout on a trail you've never run before. The chance of getting lost or hurt will increase, and the trail might not be conducive to your workout goals.

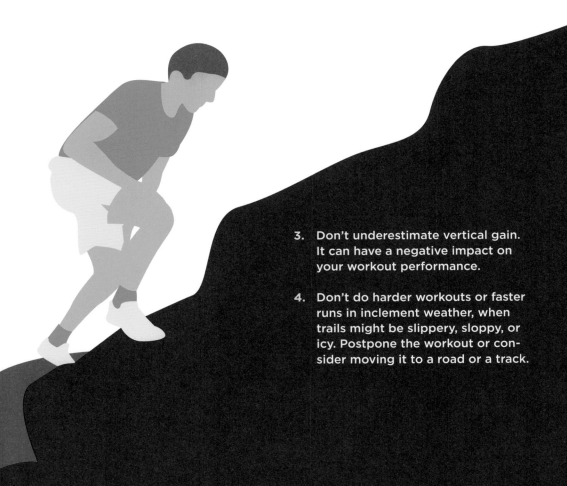

3. Don't underestimate vertical gain. It can have a negative impact on your workout performance.

4. Don't do harder workouts or faster runs in inclement weather, when trails might be slippery, sloppy, or icy. Postpone the workout or consider moving it to a road or a track.

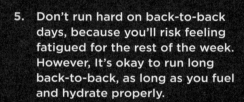

5. Don't run hard on back-to-back days, because you'll risk feeling fatigued for the rest of the week. However, It's okay to run long back-to-back, as long as you fuel and hydrate properly.

6. Don't wear the wrong shoes! While you might be able to get by with road running shoes on smooth dirt paths, make sure to wear shoes with enough flexibility, cushioning, and underfoot protection from rocks to match the trails you'll be running on.

7. Don't lose your perspective. While specific training can be helpful for improving your trail running, find-ing balance between "workouts" and regular runs is important. If you focus too much on doing specific workouts and not enjoying your time outside, you might risk burning out!

HIRE A COACH

The more you immerse yourself in training, the more you're likely to improve. But along the path to improvement, you'll encounter obstacles like training plateaus, poorly executed races, bouts of overtraining, and moments of frustration. Those are all good reasons to consider hiring a coach. A good coach will help optimize your training so you avoid common pitfalls, and will be there to hold you accountable.

You don't need to be a fast, elite runner to benefit. But keep in mind that coaches have varying training philosophies and styles. Plus, the cost of hiring a coach can range from as low as $20 a month to as high as $200. Looking for leads? Ask around, visit your local running shop, search online, take a look for a coach who trains elite trail runners, and peruse trail running training books, blogs, podcast, and videos.

Here are a few points to consider when looking for a coach:

- Does the coach have experience coaching athletes at your ability level?

- Are you okay with interaction via text and email? Or would you rather have in-person meetups with a local coach?

- How much are you willing to pay—and what do you expect to get from your investment?

- Once you've found someone you think sounds good, meet them in person or talk with them on the phone. Explain your goals and ask them about their coaching philosophy. Request references, then talk with those other clients so you can better understand how that coach manages and interacts with trail runners like you.

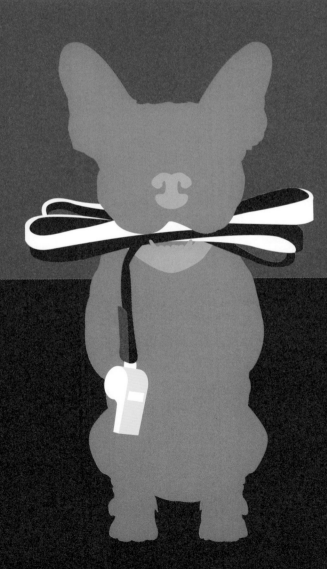

CHAPTER 6

STAYING SAFE

Ready to head for the trails? Great! One important difference between running on a trail versus a road is that it can take much longer for help to arrive if you get injured. Sometimes it's the difference between ten minutes . . . and ten hours.

Stepping away from civilization carries with it the need to be prepared, as well as have a keen understanding of self-rescue. In other words, if things go wrong, you should be able to do everything within your abilities to extricate yourself from trouble.

Fortunately, whether you're trail running in a town park or on a remote trail dozens of miles from the nearest road, the principles for staying safe are very similar. This chapter covers some of the most important points to remember.

BEFORE YOU GO: BE PREPARED

KNOW YOUR BAILOUT OPTIONS

It's important to look at a map to understand where a trail will take you and which routes it might intersect. Having your run planned is great . . . but it's also important to know your bailout options in case the weather turns nasty, you get an injury, or simply decide it's not your day and you'd rather be eating pizza on the sofa. Know your exits and how you'll get back to that sofa—as soon as you push your dog off it.

BE READY PHYSICALLY. . .

Take a look at the distance, elevation profile, and technical challenge of the route you want to run. Have you done comparable runs? Are you battling any injuries or fatigue that might reduce your ability to finish? Can you arrive at the end without feeling trashed?

When you're running off-road, help can be far away. You'll need to take care of yourself—and that means not pushing yourself to the limit because, well, you never know what's around the corner. It might be a sprained ankle, someone else in need, or a flooded river you can't cross.

KNOW THE LAND MANAGER

Most trail runs take place on public lands, and those land agencies can have widely varying rules. Check online for their guidelines. Is the trail multiuse—meaning mountain bikes or horses will be coming your way? Are all the trails open when you want to run? Is a permit required? And can you bring your four-legged sidekick?

. . . AND MENTALLY

Being mentally ready is just as important as your physical readiness. Are you going to be "psyched out" by the remoteness of a route, scared by exposure to steep terrain, or worried about wild animals? Are you feeling calm, cool, and collected . . . or downright petrified? Challenge yourself—but not so much that you're freaking out.

KNOW YOUR SOS

Add the phone number for the local rescue agency to the contacts in your phone, and know the nearest place you can go to for help. You can also consider carrying a satellite device with an SOS function. Cell phones often don't work when you're far from town, or around a ridge, so don't count on getting a signal everywhere.

And if you do whip it out to text a killer photo to your friends at work or make a call, be respectful: a lot of backcountry travelers are there to have a day away from technology, texts, and emoticons!

TAKE A FRIEND—OR TIP ONE OFF

There's nothing quite so nice as sharing the trail with a pal. When it comes to trail running, there's an extra advantage too—you can help each other if one of you gets injured. If you can't rustle up a friend, at least make sure that a trusted pal knows your route and your estimated return time.

If your run is entirely within cell coverage, Strava's Beacon feature allows someone to track your run. (There are other apps and satellite trackers, too—see Chapter 3 for the full scoop.)

If I'm going to a new area, or a place that sees very little traffic from other people, I always tell my girlfriend or someone in my family my general itinerary and when I plan to be done.
—Mike Foote, top ultrarunner from Missoula, Montana

GEAR UP

Use the info in Chapter 3 as a starting point. Then adapt it based on the unique conditions of where you're running and your preferences. For example, do you need gaiters to keep out loose scree, shoe traction devices to help you get over a high pass with fresh snow, or a filter to fill your water bottle with water—minus the bugs?

SET A TURNAROUND TIME

It's great to be committed . . . but don't get overcommitted. When you're running in terra incognita, it can be easy to misjudge how long a run will take. Pick a point that's perhaps a third of the way into your run, and set yourself a time to turn around there if you're running late. Then, stick to it! That way, if you seriously underestimated, you won't end the day wearing a dim headlamp.

CHECK THE FORECAST

Before you go, always check the latest weather forecast. If it's changed, be flexible and adjust your plans—and tweak the gear you're bringing if necessary. If you want to really geek out, ask about common weather patterns in the area where you're running. For example, in Europe's Alps, the mistral wind brings strong gusts of cold air from the north—you'll want to bundle up!

BE PREPARED TO ENCOUNTER WILD BEASTS

Trail running means you're headed into wild country—land we share with animals big and small. Before you go, find out if there are any creatures that require extra attention on your part, such as venomous snakes, mountain lions, bears, or moose.

To be a good guest, get to know their habits so you can avoid surprising those local residents. When we surprise animals, they can react defensively and threaten our safety. Are you running during rutting or nesting season? Do the local snakes like to sun themselves on south-facing ledges? If all of this has you worried, remember this: dangerous animal encounters are rare. In fact, sometimes the most frightening encounters you might have could be with the human variety.

If you do have an encounter with a wild animal, the good news is that few animals are looking for a showdown. Like you, they mostly just want to be left alone. But don't turn and hightail it out of there—that can trigger an animal's instinct to chase. Instead, back away, facing the animal but not making eye contact, which can be perceived as a threat. Talk in a gentle but clear voice that will suggest to the animal you're not a threat. You'll each have your personal space back before you know it!

IN THE LAND OF THE GRIZZLIES

In eastern Europe and the western United States and Alaska, brown bears are a concern for trail runners. US trail runner Mike Foote runs amid the "griz" from his home in Montana. "I make noise," Foote says. "I don't wear headphones. I'm aware of wind direction and if there are other natural sounds like a stream or creek which could be covering up my noise-making. I do anything I can to not surprise wildlife."

AND THE NOT-SO-WILD ONES

Here's a twist! Sometimes cows and other domestic animals are more dangerous than wild animals. Moms of all species can be protective, whether people, cows, goats, or even—yes!—geese. When provoked, cows protecting their calves have attacked and even killed passing hikers.

Give animals plenty of room, put your dog on a leash, and if you are charged, try to put a tree or fence between you and the ornery mom. In Europe's Alps, sheep "guardian" dogs who protect herds should be treated with care—they will perceive you as a threat, not a friend eager to give pats and a treat!

LIGHTING IT UP

No matter where we run, lightning can pose a risk. If, despite heeding the weather forecast and the darkening skies, a thunderstorm is in your immediate future, first try to trail run your way to a lower and safer location. If you're really, truly stuck out in an exposed spot, don't seek shelter under tall objects and don't lie on the ground. Instead, crouch on your feet, ideally in a location that provides you some protection from the elements, but doesn't stick out in the landscape.

Unsure whether that distant rumble is a real risk? Know the 30-30 rule: If you see a lightning strike and it's 30 seconds or less until you hear the rumble, the storm is near enough to be dangerous. After the storm ends, wait 30 minutes before heading off.

GOING UP—WAY, WAY UP

Some trail runs lead up—way, way up. When running at elevations above about 8000 feet (about 2500 m), most of us will start to notice the thinner air. Your heart will be beating faster, your lungs will be working harder, and you might develop a headache or feel a little "spacey." If you're not going higher than about 10,000 feet (about 3000 m), and just spending an hour or two at elevation, there's not much to worry about. However, if you are running for days at a time at higher elevations, it pays to acclimatize by spending a few days between 8000 and 10,000 feet, avoiding strenuous exercise, drinking plenty of water, and gaining altitude slowly.

WHEN IT'S TIME TO DESCEND

If you run up to 8000 feet (about 2500 m) or higher quickly and then stay there for more than half a day, you could be at risk for acute mountain sickness, or AMS, which happens when your body reacts poorly to the reduced oxygen levels. Signs and symptoms include dizziness, difficulty breathing, coughing, chest congestion, wheezing, a rapid heartbeat, confusion, extreme fatigue, and an impaired mental state. AMS can be life-threatening. Fortunately, the fix is easy: head down as soon as possible. The symptoms will usually leave just as quickly as they arrived!

DON'T BE A TARGET

In a lot of regions, trail runners find themselves sharing the land with hunters in search of deer, game birds, or even ibex and bears. Take precautions by asking the land manager whether it's hunting season. If it is, find out where hunters are likely to be located. When hunters are out, wear some blaze orange or fluorescent yellow clothing. Make noise to alert hunters in the area. And if you're still worried? Trail run somewhere else, closer to roads or an area that's more likely to be gun-free.

BE FLEXIBLE

Congrats—you're ready to head out the door! Before you go, take a moment to get your head into the game, too. The most important point is to be flexible. Adapt to changing circumstances. Being goal oriented is great most of the time—but it's not helpful if circumstances call for you to adjust your route. The old climbing adage "The mountain is always there" is a good one. You can always come back another day!

8000
FEET

ON THE TRAIL

Now you're on the trail—that's what it's all about! To maximize the fun factor, here are some tips to keep in mind as you stay safe and impress the squirrels with your trail running prowess.

COLD TO THE CORE

Not having enough warm layers can cause more than just discomfort—it can lead to hypothermia, a serious medical problem. When your body temperature drops below 95°F (35°C), you'll start shivering uncontrollably, your speech will become slurred, and your brain will get sluggish—resulting in poor decision-making. It's a recipe best avoided by getting to a warmer environment like a shelter or lower elevation, or by adding dry layers. Bring a dry base layer, and dress to minimize sweating; sweat can reduce the insulating ability of your base layer, which can also contribute to hypothermia.

OUR BREAKABLE BODY PARTS

Someday on a run, it's possible you'll get injured. Coping with an injury mid-run can be a challenge. You'll need to "self-rescue," getting yourself back to the trailhead with your own grit and ingenuity. If you can't self-rescue, call for help or send someone out for aid. Staying calm and avoiding further injury are key principles. Backcountry first aid is an important and complicated topic. To learn more, take a basic first-aid course in your area.

THOSE PESKY BLISTERS

Blisters are one of the most common—and annoying—afflictions for trail runners. If left untreated, they can slow your running to a hobble, which in itself can create other challenges for your day. The best thing to do is to never get them! Make sure your trail running shoes and socks fit you well, and before you go, treat your feet to the pleasure of an anti-chafing lubricant. Bring a change of socks if you're out for a long, hot day. If you do feel a blister forming, stop and check it out. Bring a lightweight blister treatment kit so that you can pad around the blister, reducing the friction that created it. But what if the blister is already big and hurting? Opinions vary, but our advice is to take a few minutes to pop it.

HOW TO POP A PAINFUL BLISTER

You have two goals: comfort and preventing infection. Here's how we get there!

1. Use a sterile scalpel or big, hollow-bore needle.

2. Cut an opening large enough so that the blister can drain. If you have a few minutes, allow gravity to be your friend.

3. Use an antibiotic ointment such as Bacitracin to avoid infection.

4. Cover with a sterile dressing and tape it securely.

5. Try to identify what caused the blister in the first place and adjust your shoes and socks accordingly to prevent further problems.

LISTEN TO YOUR INTUITION

Your intuition is a valuable piece of information that should not be ignored. It combines your "sixth sense" with past history, experience, and other, immeasurable qualities. Your intuition can save you from trouble when you're out on a run. "I engage with my intuition. I listen to it," says top US trail runner Hillary Allen. "Some days it doesn't feel right, and that's okay. To be flexible is important."

TAKE IT TO THE NEXT LEVEL

- Take a Wilderness First Aid course and be ready for just about any injury you encounter on the trail—whether it's your own or someone else's.

- Sign up for a Leave No Trace weekend course and dive deep into how to be a good steward in the backcountry.

- Challenge yourself by trail running someplace you wouldn't normally go and follow the steps outlined in this chapter to prepare for the adventure.

CHAPTER 7

FINDING A GREAT TRAIL— AND STAYING ON IT

You've got the gear. Maybe you've gone on a few runs on your local trails. Now it's time to explore . . . But how do you find great trails—and how do you stay on them through all those twists and turns? Read on!

In Search of Trails

FINDING YOUR PATH

Finding trails to run can be as easy as looking for green on a map, whether it's Google Maps or Apple Maps, or the old paper one you've got on a shelf somewhere. Finding trails can be easy if, for example, you live in a city or town that is located near mountains or forests, with ample nature reserves and public parks, like Boulder, Colorado, or San Francisco, California. Identify the local land agencies and check out their websites. A world of trails will open up. If you don't have a national forest at the end of your road, however, it might be time to enlist some help.

OLD SCHOOL: FIND A SHOP OR JOIN A GROUP

Your first and best source of trail info will be your nearest running shop. Even if it's 50 miles (80 km) away, chances are good they can point you toward great runs in your 'hood, and maybe even connect you with local trail runners who will have a lot of insider info.

Regional trail running groups are also great sources of information. Many are very active and filled with enthusiastic members! Take, for example, the dedicated legions belonging to the Upper Midwest Trail Runners (UMTR), or the Chicago Ultrarunners: two groups thriving in geographic regions where trail options aren't necessarily obvious. UMTR's Facebook group is full of questions from people new to the sport, or new to the area, looking for trail and race recommendations; veterans, meanwhile, often advertise their Saturday long run and invite any and all to join.

Almost all trail running clubs have a social media presence. Follow them online, and don't be afraid to ask questions. Most trail runners love sharing their passion and knowledge with newbies, so expect helpful answers. In the US, the American Trail Running Association (ATRA) maintains an online database of more than one hundred trail running clubs!

NEW SCHOOL: THERE'S AN APP FOR THAT

In addition to trail running shops and clubs, there is no shortage of cool apps you can use. Trail running apps are proliferating, and many of them are focused on aggregating trail running routes. Some of the most popular include FATMAP, Strava, RunGo, AllTrails, and Trail Run Project. Strava and FATMAP even include "heat maps" that show the relative popularity of each trail run. Cairn is a useful app that helps trail runners share running plans and pinpoints where cell coverage exists. PeakVisor is a fun and useful app that identifies peaks through the lens of your smartphone's camera.

TWO VERY DIFFERENT TRAIL RUNNING CLUBS

Chamonix, France, is often considered the world's trail running capital. And at the heart of that scene is CMBM, a trail club named after the race they helped create, the Chamonix Mont Blanc Marathon. CMBM offers twice-weekly training sessions at three different skill levels and professional coaching, and the club organizes trips to trail races. It's no wonder some of the world's best trail runners hail from this region of the Alps!

In contrast, the US has a more recent trail running club, the Trail Animals Running Club (TARC), which started online and has grown quickly. Established in the mid-1990s and now led by "Head Yeti" Bob Crowley, the group has a loyal social media following and more than 6000 members. TARC hosts a dozen trail races, and their Facebook page provides a venue for new runners to easily connect with a lively trail running community.

Staying on the Trail

HOW TO AVOID GETTING LOST

If there's one thing you want to avoid in this sport, it's losing the "trail" in your "trail run." Staying on the trail is a process that starts before you find yourself near a trail. Always study a map of where you're going. Then bring it along—both on your phone and in the form of a traditional paper map (as a backup to your phone). Unlike your phone, a paper map doesn't need to connect to a cell tower, it doesn't run on batteries, and you can drop it while you're running and it won't shatter. We also recommend that you carry a super-old-school traditional compass. It'll always function, and will keep you from walking around in circles when you're down on your luck and directionally challenged!

Smartphones, when they work, have more features than a paper map. Most mapping apps will show your current location, but be sure to download the maps you'll need so you can access them offline when cell service isn't available. Many mapping apps have additional tools—for example, precisely measuring distances between two points and offering updated trail conditions. Your phone's location service works even when you're not in range of a cell tower, so put your phone into airplane mode and save your battery in case you need it for an emergency!

Once you're at the trailhead, familiarize yourself with the key landmarks in the area and their approximate position from you. Use big features such as the coast, a railway line, a summit, a peak, or the sun to gain an overall orientation. Next, mentally note if you are running toward, along, or away from various features. At key junctions, stop and take a "mental photograph"—or better yet, a real one. It might be helpful at some point later.

CARTOGRAPHY CLASS IS IN SESSION!

Cartography is too varied and detailed a topic to give a full tutorial here. If you're not familiar with reading a map, taking the time to get a lesson from a more experienced friend is well worth it.

However, there are a few universally applicable guidelines to make your first time exploring a new trail system more enjoyable.

First, use the map scale to decipher the length of a trail. Then, use that distance—and the vertical gain or loss—to estimate how long your run will take.

Second, look for indications of the topography—the "lay of the land"—by checking out the contour lines, which indicate elevation, slope, and features like summits and valleys. The more closely spaced the contour lines, the steeper the terrain.

Look for the map key, and identify other features, like buildings, rivers, roads, trailheads, cliffs, campsites, towns, and—of course—trails. The more you can learn about a trail from a map, the more prepared you'll be for your run.

ARE YOU STILL ON THE TRAIL?

Some little-used trails can be hard to follow, and during certain times of year, such as when the leaves have fallen off the trees or there's snow on the ground, many trails can be tricky to locate. Here are a few things to look for to reassure yourself that you're still on the trail:

BLAZES

Do you see painted blazes that mark the way in front of you? (Many include some kind of trail blazing.) Good! You're en route. If not, turn around and see if you can find blazes headed in the opposite direction. Still no luck? You'll need to retrace your route—see "Got Lost?"

SIGNS OF TRAIL WORK

Almost all trails receive regular maintenance. Look for signs of trimmed branches, or downed trees that have been cut from the trail. Also keep an eye out for wooden bridges through wet areas, rock staircases to keep erosion in check, drainage ditching, and rock or wood water bars that are designed to divert water off the trail.

WEAR AND TEAR

If the trail you're on hasn't had recent maintenance, look for signs of other users. Notably, the ground should be more worn than nearby terrain, and there might be a slight indentation from years of walkers, hikers, and trail runners passing through.

Got Lost?

GET BACK TO WHERE YOU BELONG

If you go running a lot, sooner or later you're going to get lost. You'll be running along, enjoying a run with your mind wandering . . . and then, bam! Suddenly it hits you. You took a wrong turn and are on the wrong trail or, worse, off the trail entirely. Stop, take a deep breath, and stay calm. Before you do anything else, turn around and retrace your steps. Watch the ground for signs of the trail and look for blazes on the trees. Chances are good you'll be back on the trail within a few minutes.

In 2016, one of the world's fastest trail runners, Jim Walmsley, was far in front of the pack, crushing the course record in California's 100-mile (161 km) Western States Endurance Run, one of the most famous trail races in the world. Guess what? He made a wrong turn . . . and kept going. For 2 miles. An hour later, Walmsley turned around, ran back to the trail, and continued on to finish in nineteenth place.

. . . AND IF YOU DIDN'T FIND THE TRAIL

If you've backtracked and still can't find the trail, it might be time to hunker down. Stay put, and if you have cell coverage, dial the local emergency number you wisely added to your contacts. Got zero bars of coverage? Stay cool. In time, that trustworthy friend with whom you left your running route will call for help. If you have to spend the night out, put on your extra layers and start those jumping jacks to stay warm.

TAKE IT TO THE NEXT LEVEL

Both map use and staying safe when you're lost are expansive topics—
ones we can't do justice to in just one chapter. (Entire books have been
written on them!) If you end up spending a lot of time outdoors trail
running, climbing, or hiking, we encourage you to consider taking an
outdoor safety course, where you'll learn—among many other skills—how
to get through an unplanned night in the backcountry. If you want to
become a pro with maps, take a cartography class, or even learn to ori-
enteer and move overland without trails at all, following just a compass
bearing.

CHAPTER 8

STAYING HEALTHY AND AVOIDING INJURIES

Trail running can be a simple and enriching activity, but it can also be stressful on the body. And when stresses add up, we get injured.

It's easy to think that we get stronger while we trail run—and we do!—but in fact the opposite is also true. After a certain point, training is both building you up and breaking you down. It is only with rest that the magic happens.

If your body gets overly stressed, or if your recovery is inadequate, the breakdown processes might overwhelm your ability to heal. Overuse injuries are unfortunate consequences of a fun sport that rewards strategically stressful behavior.

By practicing injury prevention and self-care, you can minimize your risk of breakdown—and continue building up your running strength.

Before, During, and After Your Trail Run

If all you do is run, you are not doing enough. Trail running's beautiful simplicity attracts many people, but if you make it too simple, there is a risk that your body won't be prepared to experience the beauty. The following tips and exercises will help you stay healthy on the trails.

1. BEFORE YOU RUN

A good warm-up routine can prevent many injuries. The key is to focus on dynamic movements and mobility, rather than the stretching you may have done in gym class.

The benefits of a warm-up are threefold:

- First, it improves range of motion and prepares the joints and muscles for the dynamic movements that happen while running. Muscles that were dormant will now be ready for action!

- Second, it gets the blood pumping and literally warms up extremities, making them more resilient at the beginning of the run.

- Third, by starting your physiological engine, it reduces perceived exertion at the start of the run, giving you more bang for your running buck.

So how should you warm up? The options are endless, but a tried-and-true routine is to mix easy lunges, leg swings, arm swings, and fast walking over the course of five minutes. But almost anything will work, so get creative. Some runners even swear by dancing prior to their early morning runs! Moving your hips and torso is one way to prepare for grooving on the trail.

THE 5-MINUTE WARM-UP

Let's set the scene. You drive up to the trailhead. You're groggy from not quite enough sleep, stressed from work, or sore from a previous day's workout. What do you do? Here's a warm-up routine designed to get you ready for running by awakening your mind and activating your neuromuscular timing.

MINUTE 1: WALK BRISKLY

Fast walking will get your blood flowing, your muscles warm, and your mind ready for what comes next.

MINUTE 2: FORWARD AND REAR LUNGES

Lunges open up the hips and get your heart beating faster, plus they warm up the hamstring and quadriceps muscle groups. After a set of ten easy forward and rear lunges, you should start feeling more alert and ready to run. But watch out—these might be challenging the first few times you do them.

MINUTE 3: SIDE-TO-SIDE LUNGES AND TIPTOE WALK

Doing ten side-to-side lunges will warm up and gently stretch the groin muscles, hips, and iliotibial band in a different plane of motion than it may be used to. Start with your legs together and your hands on your hips. Next, alternate extending one leg to the side and following it with the other leg back to the neutral starting position. These multi-plane movements can help guard against overuse injuries by engaging more muscles, allowing you to be more dynamic as you adjust to the variability of the terrain. That will reduce your body's reliance on the same muscle groups for every stride. For the rest of the minute, walk on your toes to activate and warm your calves and Achilles tendons, which will help prevent any sudden movements from causing tearing once you start.

MINUTE 4: FRONT-TO-BACK AND SIDE-TO-SIDE LEG SWINGS

Leg swings are the best way to mimic running motion without actually bearing any weight. Do ten in each direction, relaxing your hip and letting your foot go through the entire range of motion, dynamically stretching the hip flexors and hamstrings. Warning: Don't swing so high that it hurts!

MINUTE 5: SLOW JOGGING

The final step is to slowly jog around —a few minutes per mile slower than you plan on starting your run. A quick bounce-around lets your body get used to the pounding, while also letting you know if there are any minor ailments that might prevent you from running. Since most major injuries start out as minor problems, it's worth paying close attention to the signals from your body during this brief jog.

2. DURING YOUR RUN

Once you start running, start slow and take a mental inventory of how your body is feeling. Most running injuries don't just happen—chronic overuse injuries are far more common than acute ailments like ankle sprains or a torn ACL (the anterior cruciate ligament in your knee). They often start as a nagging concern but blossom into a full-blown problem over many miles.

EASE IN!

A good warm-up is super important if you are going to be doing a higher-intensity trail run. Many runners (you know who you are!) want to jump right into the hard stuff, especially if you have one eye on your watch. Allow yourself 15–20 minutes of low-intensity jogging, then do a few exercises, then run a bit faster for 10 minutes, with some bursts of speed mixed in.

How do you know the difference between a pain you should run through and something you shouldn't? The answer isn't simple, but the general rule is to err on the side of caution. When in doubt, stop your run and survive to run another day. No one regrets cutting a run a few miles short to prevent injury, but a lot of people regret running a few miles too far!

3. AFTER YOUR RUN

Just like how a good warm-up can prevent injuries before they happen, a good cooldown and strengthening routine can keep your body resilient against training stress. Immediately after your run, do some more leg swings and light stretching while your body is warm. Hydrate, refuel, and take a minute or two to put your feet up and decompress from the run, if possible. These little actions can help prepare your body for the rest of your day.

DESK TRAINING

Many trail runners have to spend eight to ten hours working in an office each day, which means relative inactivity for most of the day. If that describes you, don't despair. With these strategic exercises, you can use that time for recovery and adaptation.

1. WALK AROUND
Every hour, set your watch to remind you to walk around for 5 to 10 minutes. Walk briskly, as if there is an urgent meeting down the hall. (Added bonus? Your colleagues will assume you're doing something very important!)

2. STAND UP
Every 20 minutes, stand up and move your hips forward to engage your glutes and relax your hip flexors. This motion looks rather suggestive, so be careful where and how you do it, unless you want to be reported to your boss for lewd behavior. A standing desk is another option if it works for you. If you want to go really hardcore, talk your boss into a walking treadmill desk during your next employee review!

3. FOOT CIRCLES

Every 10 minutes, do ten to twenty foot circles in both directions. Keeping your legs engaged will help keep your blood flowing.

4. PUSH-UPS

When you hit that afternoon lull, do a set of push-ups, and planks if you're game for them. These exercises will get your blood flowing and can release hormones that speed up the healing process.

5. NEED A BIT OF DISCIPLINE? TOMATOES TO THE RESCUE!

The Pomodoro Technique, named for the tomato-shaped timer used by the originator of the idea, is a specific routine that can help you stay active during the workday. It involves setting a timer to do focused work for 25-minute intervals, after which you take a 5-minute break. Get up, walk around, stretch your legs—or choose another form of light exercise that works for you. After four cycles, you get a 15-minute break. There are even apps and desktop browser add-ons based on this technique. Try it out!

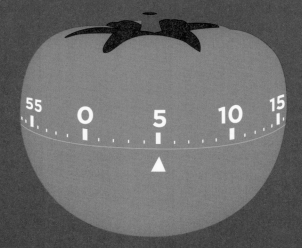

NEVER STOP HYDRATING

We go out of our way to bring water or a sports drink on a run, but we often neglect good hydration practices for the rest of the day. If you're not drinking enough fluids throughout your workday, you'll inhibit your workouts and slow your recovery. You'll benefit immensely if you make it a habit to sip from a water bottle every fifteen minutes while you're at work.

REST IS BEST

You can do everything right and still get injured, sick, or fatigued. The nature of life and running is that things aren't always linear and predictable. In an unpredictable world, it's essential to learn to anticipate and adapt. The moral of the story, which applies just as well to your weekly trail running, is to exercise diligently, then make sure your body gets enough rest. Rest comes in two forms: first, taking a break from running a couple of days per week, and second, making sure you're getting enough sleep to allow your body to recover and restore itself.

AVOIDING MENTAL BURNOUT

There's a good chance you'll really like trail running once you get into it. In fact, you might like it a lot—so much so that you'll want to run every day, set new goals, run new trails, and try new races. Those are all great things and, in fact, they're also our goals for you in writing this book. But it's equally important to stay grounded and not become obsessive about the sport.

How do you keep from falling off the deep end? Here's our advice:

- Don't overdo it on the training.

- Set realistic race goals.

- Make time for an off-season in which you take a break from trail running for at least two or three weeks. This might mean doing other activities, such as hiking, biking, swimming, or spending some regular time in the gym. Or do nothing at all. Take a vacation and put any thoughts about trail running on hold.

Taking a break will help rejuvenate you, physically and mentally. And it will rekindle your love for trail running.

FOAM ROLL, EVERY DAY

At some point every day—for example, right after your run, in a conference room at work, or before you go to bed—do at least five minutes of work with a firm foam roller, focusing on your quads, calves, hips, and hamstrings. Foam rolling releases built-up tension and tightness, helping prevent some injuries like IT (iliotibial) band syndrome, while simultaneously making your legs feel fresher each day. Even if you're just running a couple of times a week, make sure you're diligently using a foam roller.

TIPS TO AVOID OVERUSE INJURIES

1. Run different types of trails during any given week. Your body will appreciate the variety.

2. Don't wear the same pair of shoes every time you go trail running. Alternating pairs will keep both your feet and your physique fresh.

3. If your shoes make your feet hurt or make you feel awkward, it's time for new shoes.

4. Do a functional strength routine, yoga, or CrossFit at least twice a week to strengthen your core and the associated stabilizing muscles.

5. Take at least one or two days off a week from running—including one complete day of rest—to help your body recover. On other non-running days, consider cross-training to give your body a bit of a break while still exercising.

THE BENEFITS OF CROSS-TRAINING

As much as we love to run, we don't do it every day. It's important to give your body a break from the pounding and repetitive stress that comes with regularly running moderate to long distances. Indulge in a bit of cross-training a couple of days per week with yoga, cycling, Nordic skiing, skinning uphill on skis, rowing, swimming, or hiking. These kinds of low-impact activities allow a workout without the pounding and jarring of trail running. They're a great option for trail runners who are prone to overuse injuries—and an excellent way to keep the endorphins flowing if you are injured!

DO SOME PRE-HAB

No matter how fit or strong we are, we're bound to have physical weaknesses and gait deficiencies that can lead to aches and pains from time to time. How can you manage that? Visit a local physical therapist that trail runners you know recommend, and get exercises and drills prescribed for you that are specifically tailored to your unique anatomy and gait idiosyncracies. Do those exercises and drills relentlessly, even if any lingering soreness or aches disappear. Then schedule a follow-up appointment 90 days later, just on principle. You can always cancel it if you're feeling 100 percent, but chances are you'll be glad you have that appointment when it does roll around.

CHAPTER 9

HELP— SOMETHING HURTS!

Even if you train well, get the right gear, and are extra careful out on the trails, you're still not going to avoid injuries entirely. Maybe you trip and fall, or your training adds a bit too much stress and some part of your body begins to ache. Run enough, and sooner or later something will hurt. You'll have your first trail running injury.

Almost all trail running injuries fall into one of two general categories: traumatic injuries or overuse injuries.

Traumatic Injuries

Traumatic injuries are the ones that happen when you land on the ground too hard or awkwardly. Ankle sprains, pulled hamstrings, and stubbed toes are the most common types of injuries in that category, as the variable conditions of the trail can often make your foot placements unstable.

Other traumatic injuries can occur when you trip and fall, kick a rock with one of your feet, or slip on a muddy or icy patch of trail. These kinds of accidents have been known to result in everything from painfully scraped ankles to bone bruises on the bottoms of your feet, fingers, ankles, ribs, and forearms, and sometimes even concussions.

If you do get a traumatic injury while trail running, the most important thing is to not make it worse. Stop and assess your situation, and see if you need any immediate interventions, such as stopping some bleeding. You might need to slowly walk back to the trailhead with the help of a friend. Or if you cannot self-rescue, you might even need to call for a rescue. What's important is your immediate well-being. Remember that many injuries will slowly get worse over the ensuing few hours, so proceed conservatively. You can always come back and run another day! (See Chapter 6 for info on staying safe.) When in doubt, head to an emergency clinic or your local hospital to get your injury checked out.

HOW TO AVOID TRIPPING

1. Be alert! Always scan the trail several steps ahead of your feet.

2. Identify obstacles that might become an issue, such as rocks, roots, ice, or mud. Have a plan to dodge them or handle them gracefully.

3. Maintain good upright running form, focusing on shorter strides and agility.

4. If you start to wobble, spread your arms wide to maintain balance.

5. Never wear shoes with worn-out outsole treads. That's a recipe for disaster!

6. If it's icy or snowy, run in spiked shoes or wear removable traction devices.

7. Stay optimally fueled and hydrated. Falling often occurs when your focus wanes as your blood sugar declines.

8. If you're running at dawn or dusk, wear a headlamp so you can see what's on the trail in front of you.

9. For some trail runners, the most common place to trip, fall, or sprain an ankle is at the end of a run, when you're close to home or the trailhead. Extra vigilance is necessary when your run is almost over. Continue to stay focused on your run, and don't rush to finish!

LEARN TO FALL

Tripping and falling is inevitable when you're trail running. You can't always avoid it, but you can minimize the damage by learning how to fall defensively and safely. According to Max King, a professional trail runner from Bend, Oregon, the key in most instances is to prepare to tuck and roll as soon as you feel yourself stumbling toward the ground. Rolling avoids direct impact with the ground and protects your fingers, forearms, and head. (Do we need to say it? Avoid crashing headfirst at all costs.) Most experienced trail runners will tell you the tuck-and-roll technique is learned habit that becomes instinctual. "It's not something you want to practice, but if you can train yourself to roll to avoid direct impact with the ground or a rock, you're probably going to be much better off," King says.

Overuse Injuries

The majority of road running injuries are caused from the repetitive motion of a runner's gait. Fortunately, the softer and more variable surfaces of trails can help reduce the prevalence of some of those injuries. However, running on trails doesn't make us immune to achy legs, knees, and ankles.

Here's a rundown of the most common overuse injuries in trail running. We recommend taking time off, using RICE treatments (see page 148), and visiting a doctor or physical therapist if symptoms linger for more than a week.

LOWER BACK SORENESS/PAIN

Seriousness

Trail running can put a lot of strain on your lower back because the muscles in that region are often called upon to help keep the body stable as it twists and wobbles on arduous climbs, steep descents, and uneven terrain. However, if the pain feels abnormal, it can be indicative of a serious ailment, so get it checked out! The more core strength you develop, the less lower back soreness will trouble you.

IT BAND SYNDROME

Seriousness

If you experience pain and tenderness on the outer part of your thigh and knee, it's likely inflammation or stretching of the iliotibial band. This occurs when the muscles on one side of your body pull your hips and legs out of alignment, causing the IT band to be stretched uncomfortably.

RUNNER'S KNEE

Seriousness

Known to the cognoscenti as patello-femoral pain syndrome, this problem occurs when you put additional stress on your knee by running a lot more or a lot faster in training before your body is ready for it.

SHIN SPLINTS

Seriousness

The technical term for this is medial tibial stress syndrome, a very painful throbbing of the front of your lower leg that occurs when you do too much running and too many hard workouts too soon. The increased activity creates microtears in the overworked muscles, tendons, and bone tissue. Warning! If you keep running, a very serious tibial stress fracture could be next.

ACHILLES SORENESS

Seriousness

This mild to acute soreness along the Achilles tendon at the back of your ankle and lower calf is called Achilles tendinitis. It's usually caused by stiff feet or tight calf muscles. The tendon becomes inflamed if your body is out of balance or you're favoring one side on long runs or steep climbs.

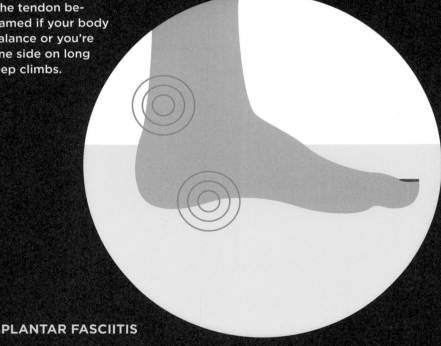

PLANTAR FASCIITIS

Seriousness

Plantar fasciitis is an achy feeling directly under your heel. It's caused by inflammation and/or microtearing of the plantar fascia or the long plantar ligament in the foot. It is most commonly caused by stretching of the plantar fascia due to excessive pronation, which is the normal inward roll of your foot when you land. "PF" can also be caused by trail shoes that lack support.

PATELLAR TENDINITIS

Seriousness

Patellar tendinitis is a painful inflammation of the tendon that connects your kneecap, or patella, to your shinbone. The patellar tendon works with the muscles at the front of your thigh to extend your knee so that you can run and jump.

STRESS FRACTURES

Seriousness

Stress fractures occur when excess load or stress causes a tiny crack in a bone. Joints on the lower half of your body are particularly at risk for stress fractures, including your feet, ankles, and lower legs. Stress fractures can develop into full-blown fractures if you try to run through the pain.

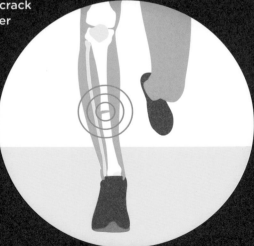

147

DO YOU WANT RICE WITH THAT?

Many injuries, and in particular sprains and strains, are best initially treated with the tried-and-true RICE method, which stands for . . .

R **is for Rest**
Take time off from running and other intense forms of exercise to let any inflammation and swelling subside.

I **is for Ice**
The cold topic of whether to use ice is currently a hot topic! Whether to use ice depends on your goals. If you sprain your ankle a few days before an important trail race, ice will help decrease the swelling and pain for the race. However, icing may slow down long-term healing, or may have no benefit at all, at least according to recent studies.

C **is for Compression**
Wrap the injured area with an elastic medical bandage, like an ACE bandage, to prevent swelling. You want it to be snug but not too tight. If it's too tight, it'll interrupt blood flow.

E **is for Elevation**
This entails raising the sore body part above the level of your heart to reduce pain, throbbing, and swelling.

MEDICATE CAREFULLY

Your doctor may suggest using nonsteroidal anti-inflammatory drugs (NSAIDs), such as ibuprofen and naproxen, along with the RICE treatment. These medicines are available over the counter and by prescription. Be careful and never use more than the recommended dosage. Studies have shown that excessive use of NSAIDs before, during, and after long runs or races when you are dehydrated can slow healing and increase the risk of acute kidney injuries.

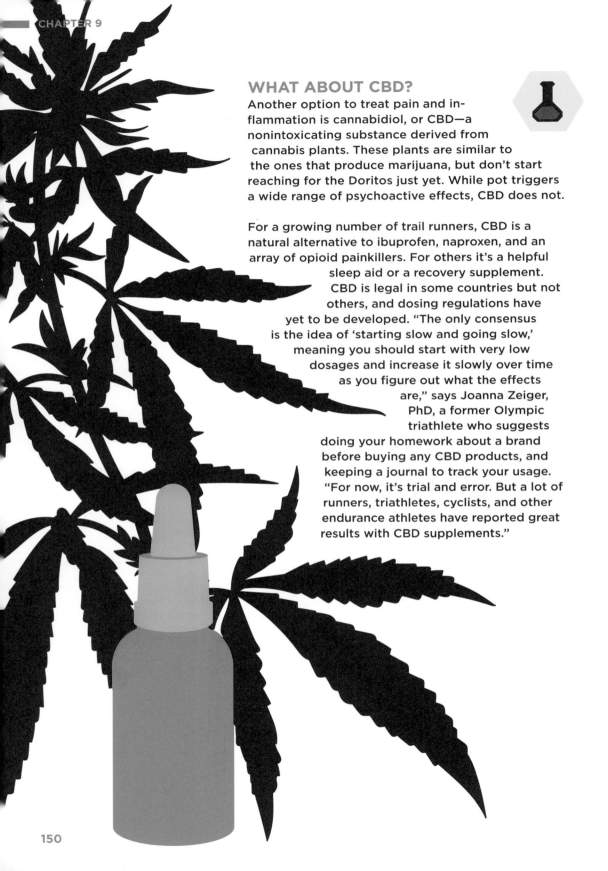

WHAT ABOUT CBD?

Another option to treat pain and inflammation is cannabidiol, or CBD—a nonintoxicating substance derived from cannabis plants. These plants are similar to the ones that produce marijuana, but don't start reaching for the Doritos just yet. While pot triggers a wide range of psychoactive effects, CBD does not.

For a growing number of trail runners, CBD is a natural alternative to ibuprofen, naproxen, and an array of opioid painkillers. For others it's a helpful sleep aid or a recovery supplement. CBD is legal in some countries but not others, and dosing regulations have yet to be developed. "The only consensus is the idea of 'starting slow and going slow,' meaning you should start with very low dosages and increase it slowly over time as you figure out what the effects are," says Joanna Zeiger, PhD, a former Olympic triathlete who suggests doing your homework about a brand before buying any CBD products, and keeping a journal to track your usage. "For now, it's trial and error. But a lot of runners, triathletes, cyclists, and other endurance athletes have reported great results with CBD supplements."

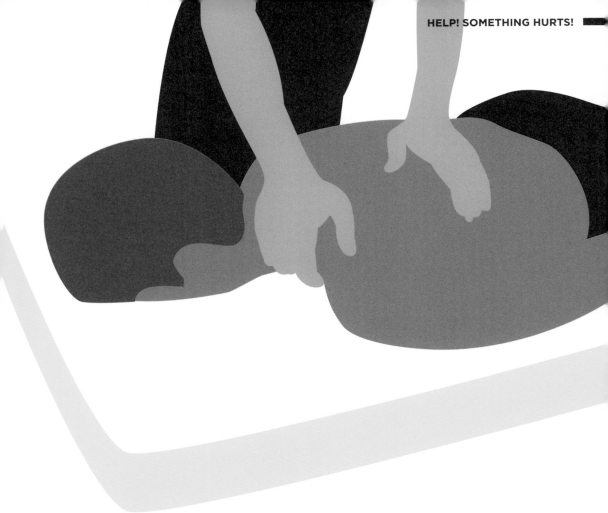

GET REGULAR MAINTENANCE

Regular trail running will invigorate your soul, your mind, and your body. But while it will make you feel stronger, it can also make you feel sore, fatigued, and broken down. Some of that is normal, but some of it will need your attention, too. It's a good practice to keep a mental inventory of the things that ail you, and to get maintenance work when necessary. Most of those ailments will probably be minor, and can be worked out with stretching, foam rolling, and other light treatments. Make sure any acute pain or lingering soreness doesn't turn into something more problematic. Visiting a running-focused physical therapist or a massage therapist on occasion can be a good way to keep your body in tip-top condition. Just as your car needs a tune-up from time to time, your body needs maintenance, too!

CHAPTER 10

WOMEN ON THE TRAILS

In years past, trail running was an overwhelmingly male sport. In subtle and not-so-subtle ways, women encountered barriers to entry and equal participation. Trail running gear was designed for men, race prizes were unequal, and women's needs—such as managing their periods—were often ignored.

All that's changing, thanks to race directors, coaches, other sport leaders, and groups like Trail Sisters and Free to Run, who are working to break down barriers and right past wrongs. In 2001, just 26 percent of participants in trail races were women; today that number is 42 percent. That's progress, but more is needed.

The advice elsewhere in this book is universally applicable to men and women. In this chapter, written by noted ultrarunner, writer, and mom Yitka Winn, we cover situations often encountered by women trail runners. No matter your gender, we encourage you to read on, if not for yourself, then for your fellow trail runner.

Why Women Run Trails

The benefits of trail running are pretty universal. Here are just a few of the (many!) reasons to be a trail runner:

- Enjoyment of being in nature

- Endorphin high of exercise

- Health benefits

- Sense of challenge and accomplishment

- Camaraderie of the trail running community

- Ability to consume calories more freely than your non-exercising peers

While runners of any gender can relate to the above, statistics show that even in our modern society, women spend more time on average than men do on household chores and childcare duties—so some might argue that women especially stand to benefit from a bit of "me time" in the form of a trail run.

Plus, in a society that still often has subtle (or not-so-subtle) expectations for how women should look, dress, and act, getting a bit muddy and adventurous in the wild is just plain fun!

A (VERY) BRIEF HISTORY OF WOMEN'S RUNNING

Following the 800-meter race at the 1928 Olympics, the *New York Times* reported that the women athletes had "plainly demonstrated that even this distance makes too great a call on feminine strength." Doctors routinely warned women their ovaries might fall out if they exercised too vigorously. It wasn't until 1972 that women were able to run longer than 800 meters in the Olympics, and it took another twelve years before a women's marathon was added to the Games.

How times have changed! Today, more than half of all road runners are female. Women's participation in trail running has followed a similar trajectory, albeit a bit further behind on the timeline. More men still participate in trail races—even more disproportionately at ultra distances—but female participation continues to rise each year.

WOMEN OF THE DIPSEA

When America's oldest trail race, California's Dipsea, prohibited women from participating, an all-female version of the race was created in 1918. It frequently drew even more participants than the men's edition! By 1950, women began "crashing" the men's race; in 1971, women were formally admitted into it.

ARLENE PIEPER: A TRAIL RUNNING PIONEER

In 1959, eight years before Kathrine Switzer made history by famously becoming the first registered female finisher of the Boston Marathon, 29-year-old Arlene Pieper completed Colorado's Pikes Peak Marathon. Competing against a field of twelve men at a time when women were not encouraged to run races, Pieper ran up and down the 14,115-foot mountain in 9 hours and 16 minutes. Her effort is one of the earliest known records of a woman running a trail marathon.

WOMEN DOMINATE

The longer women run, the more likely the chance they'll outrun the men. At least that's the trend of some elite runners who have seemingly made long-held gender biases irrelevant. Take for example Courtney Dauwalter, a trail runner from Golden, Colorado, who is one of the strongest trail ultramarathoners anywhere. She's won more than ten ultras outright—meaning she beat all of the men, too—and in 2017 she won the 240-mile (386 km) Moab Endurance Run in Utah, by almost 10 hours. "I definitely prefer the longer, harder races, both physically and mentally," Dauwalter has said. "I just think they're more interesting."

In 2019, American Maggie Guterl won Big's Backyard Ultra in Tennessee, a unique race that consists of running consecutive 4.167-mile (6.7 km) loops to exhaustion. To win the race, she had to be the last competitor still moving. Guterl ultimately outlasted Hong Kong's Will Hayward, finishing 60 laps—and covering 250 miles (402 km)—to Hayward's 59 laps and 245.83 miles (395.6 km).

Common Barriers Women Face

Why don't more women run on the trails—especially when it comes to longer distances? Here are a few reasons that women commonly cite:

- Lack of time

- Lack of trail access

- Lack of resources or knowledge (e.g., how to handle peeing or menstruation in the backcountry)

- Lack of community

- Concerns about being attacked, falling, or getting lost while running alone

Of course, most of these can apply to anyone, not just women.

WHAT WOMEN WANT

Not all women agree on the best way to get more women involved in trail running or whether, for that matter, such a goal is even necessary. Some believe their fellow ladies do not need to be encouraged (or coddled) to run trails. One of the fun aspects of trail running, after all, is that unlike many other organized athletic pursuits, women and men compete alongside each other. We hope that, with time, the sport will see more female participation.

NO BOYS ALLOWED

Nonetheless, some believe in taking more proactive steps to encourage other women to try trail running. This has given rise to a number of women-specific trail running clubs, events, and races, which can provide a sense of camaraderie, empowerment, and fun social time. (Many of these also aim to be inclusive of non-binary, gender-nonconforming, and trans women runners.)

If this sounds up your alley, don't hesitate to reach out to any local women's trail running groups in your area. The world is full of friendly, badass women eager to share the gospel of their sport with novices!

MEET YOUR TRAIL SISTERS

Colorado runner Gina Lucrezi founded Trail Sisters, a global community of women trail runners, with the mission of increasing women's participation and opportunities in the sport. At TrailSisters.net, you can find an amazing treasure trove of articles written by and for women trail runners, as well as a directory of local Trail Sisters groups offering beginner-friendly, no-drop group runs, a series of women's trail running retreats, adventure grants, films, trail races, female coaches, and much more.

RUNNING ALONE: THE RISKS AND REWARDS

Overcoming fears associated with being alone in the outdoors can be highly empowering. Solitary trail runs offer many gifts. They can be exhilarating, adventurous, relaxing, meditative, and intensely rewarding—often all in the same run!

Still, there are some inherent risks to running alone—but most are unrelated to gender. Here are a few common concerns and how to counteract them:

- **Worried about wildlife?** If you're not running with a friend or group, make your own noise—sing, talk, whistle, whoop, occasionally call out, "Hey, bear!" The human voice is one of the most effective tools for scaring off bears or mountain lions.

- **Nervous about falling?** A companion is probably the best insurance for a twisted ankle or other acute injury, but if you're flying solo, be sure to pack a small first-aid kit, an ACE elastic bandage, and a phone or satellite beacon to call for help in case of emergency.

- **Anxious about human predators?** Take comfort in knowing that these are statistically far less common in wilderness areas than in urban environs. Consider taking a self-defense course or carrying pepper spray for additional peace of mind, and skip the earbuds so you can be alert to your surroundings.

How to Pee in the Woods

First, find a spot away from the trail and any water sources. (But don't get lost by venturing farther away than necessary!) Watch out for poison ivy/oak, cacti, sharp pine needles, brambles, stinging nettles, or other texturally unsavory plants before you pop a squat.

Keep your stream short and splatter-free by squatting all the way down, with your butt directly behind your heels, just inches off the ground, and aiming downhill.

METHOD 1: DRIP AND DRY

Wait a few moments to air-dry as much as possible (give yourself a good shake to help things along) before pulling your pants back up.

METHOD 2: USE PLANTS

Broad plant leaves make terrific natural toilet paper. (Before doing so, be sure you can identify and avoid any poisonous ones in your area.)

METHOD 3: BYOTP

If you prefer to wipe with actual toilet paper, follow Leave No Trace principles by packing it out: seal up used toilet paper in a small ziplock baggie, and dispose of it later in a trash can.

METHOD 4: USE A PEE RAG

Wipe with a bandana or handkerchief, then tie it to the outside of your hydration pack. It will dry naturally as you run, and you can wash it later at home.

METHOD 5: USE A PEE FUNNEL

These magical little pieces of plastic allow you to pee standing up. Female urination devices take some practice to master, so try them at home in the shower before attempting to use one in the wild.

For gender-neutral advice on how to poop in the woods, see Chapter 12.

THAT TIME OF THE MONTH

Here's the good news: there's no need to dread your period, even if you have long training runs or a race on the calendar. Studies have consistently shown that menstruation has no significant effect on athletic performance.

DEALING WITH CRAMPS

Even though it may be hard to get motivated, running can actually help alleviate cramps. A few tips to get you out the door:

- Do some abdominal stretches.

- Apply a heat pad to your belly for several minutes.

- Drink plenty of water, and avoid alcohol.

- Don't hesitate to slow down or take walking breaks during your run.

- Use NSAIDs (such as aspirin, ibuprofen, and naproxen) sparingly, if at all.

HANDLING YOUR PERIOD ON LONG TRAIL RUNS

Need to change out a pad or tampon during your run? Stash two small baggies in your running pack—one with fresh supplies, sanitary wipes or toilet paper, and a small container of hand sanitizer, and the other to use as a trash bag to pack out your used supplies.

A TRAIL RUNNER'S BEST FRIEND: REUSABLE MENSTRUAL CUPS

These silicone, bell-shaped products can provide up to twelve hours of leak-free protection—enough to last the duration of most trail running adventures, so you won't have to worry about changing anything on the go. But if you do need to change it in the woods, no sweat! Just dig a proper cat hole away from water sources and empty your cup's contents. Wipe the cup as clean as possible with toilet paper or a wipe before reinserting, then wash your hands with sanitizer. Pack out any trash.

Finding a Good Sports Bra

 Forget about shoes being a runner's most critical piece of gear. Any woman can tell you that nothing can make or break a run like the fit and quality of a sports bra!

TIPS FOR GETTING A GOOD FIT

- When consulting product reviews, get your recommendations from similarly proportioned reviewers.

- If possible, get measured at a store (while wearing a regular bra) to ensure you're trying on the right size.

- When you try on a bra in a store dressing room, jog in place or do some jumping jacks to test the bra's support level.

- If the fabric has wrinkles when you try it on, it's probably too big. If it doesn't adequately cover your bosom, it's probably too small.

- If a bra band has multiple sets of hooks to fasten it, buy the one that fits snugly on the loosest set of hooks. (As it stretches out over time, you can snug up the fit by using the second or third set of hooks.)

BRA TLC

Once you've found a running bra you do love, take good care of it. If possible, wash it by hand and hang or lay it flat to dry; washing machines and dryers are hard on the elastic and can dramatically reduce your bra's life span.

WHEN TO RETIRE YOUR BRA

When your bra starts losing its support or begins chafing your skin regularly (often a product of sweat/salt buildup in the fabric over time), it's time to purchase a fresh one.

Women runners should be aware of a few health concerns specific to their bodies that can affect their performance on the trail and overall health.

IRON DEFICIENCY

In part because of menstruation, women are more susceptible to iron-deficiency anemia than men. Certain restrictive diets common among endurance athletes (such as veganism, vegetarianism, and gluten-free diets) can put women at additional risk.

Iron deficiency can manifest as a host of symptoms detrimental to running performance, including fatigue, weakness, dizziness, shortness of breath, irregular heartbeat, and cold hands or feet. If any of these sound familiar, schedule a doctor's visit to get a complete blood test done. Treatment may include iron supplements and/or dietary changes.

IMPORTANT TO KNOW!

Regular use of pain relievers can also cause internal bleeding in the stomach that further depletes iron.

FEMALE ATHLETE TRIAD

Although eating disorders can affect anyone of any gender, there is one related concern that is specific to women. Dubbed the "female athlete triad," or just the "Triad" for short, this is a syndrome based on three related conditions that often occur at the same time:

- Energy deficiency, often related to disordered eating
- Amenorrhea, or lack of menstrual periods
- Diminished bone density, including osteoporosis and stress fractures

See a doctor if you are experiencing one or more of the Triad conditions.

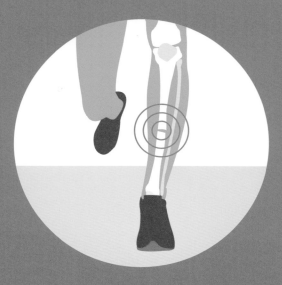

Taking a Pregnant Pause

Pregnancy is an amazing, life-changing experience, but it sometimes means you'll have to reduce your trail running, or in some situations take a break altogether. If you're a frequent runner and your identity is closely linked to your community built around running, racing, or adventuring with others, pregnancy can lead to a challenging transition.

STAY POSITIVE

Don't get hung up on what your body *can't* do. Focus instead on what it *can*, and is, doing—it's producing a human! That's a pretty big deal. Think about how special it is to get to bring a child into the world—and how lucky your future offspring will be to grow up with such an active, outdoorsy role model. A year, or even a few years, is a blink of the eye in the timeline of life.

TRAINING WHILE PREGNANT

The good news is that if you are a healthy woman with a low-risk pregnancy, you should be able to continue running throughout your pregnancy. In fact, most doctors will strongly encourage you to exercise regularly! Doing so not only helps keep your health in check but also reduces your risk for many pregnancy-related conditions.

Plus, trail running can be a terrific mental break—an opportunity to relax, clear your mind, and spend quality time outdoors with your unborn child. Here are our tips for trail running while pregnant:

- Invest in a belly band, which is like a sports bra for your stomach.

- Consider wearing compression socks to aid in blood flow to your lower extremities.

- Make peace with running at a lower intensity than you're accustomed to.

- Beware of comparing yourself to other pregnant runners on social media; every woman's pregnancy journey is unique.

- A few things to avoid on runs: overheating, extremely technical terrain, and venturing too far into the backcountry during your third trimester. Additionally, check with your doctor before running at high altitude (8500+ feet/2600+ m) if it's significantly higher than where you reside.

EMBRACE CHANGE

Pregnancy means relinquishing some of the control that you, as an athlete, are probably accustomed to exerting over your body. Welcome the opportunity to rest more. If you can't participate in races, then consider volunteering at some to stay connected to your community. If running isn't possible (or at least not at the same intensities), embrace the chance to explore other interests—maybe hiking or other, lower-impact activities like swimming and cross-country skiing or ski touring. Take the time to catch up with your non-runner friends, or read all those books you never had time for when your life revolved around running. Look at this time as an opportunity to do something new.

POSTPARTUM RUNNING

Some women bounce back from pregnancy right away, but many don't. Aside from the sleep deprivation of rearing an infant, not-uncommon complications like pelvic floor injuries, diastasis recti (abdominal separation), recovery from a caesarean section, incontinence, or postpartum depression can make it hard to get back into running.

Many women take a lot of time off—sometimes by choice, sometimes not. Be patient with your own journey. Rely on your support systems. Have faith that even if it doesn't happen right away, running can and will be a part of your life again, if you want it to be. Like many women, you may find yourself developing an even more meaningful relationship with the sport than you had before.

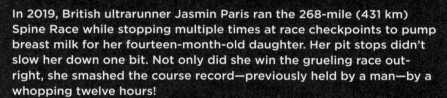

BABY POWER

In 2019, British ultrarunner Jasmin Paris ran the 268-mile (431 km) Spine Race while stopping multiple times at race checkpoints to pump breast milk for her fourteen-month-old daughter. Her pit stops didn't slow her down one bit. Not only did she win the grueling race outright, she smashed the course record—previously held by a man—by a whopping twelve hours!

Menopause

The average age for American women to experience menopause is 51 years. Given that many women trail run well into their 50s, 60s, 70s, and sometimes even 80s, managing the challenges of menopause as an athlete is a task many women will face at some point in their lives.

The good news is that studies have shown that running can help alleviate common symptoms of menopause such as sleep disruptions, hot flashes, mood swings, and weight gain.

Weight-bearing exercise and strength training also help build and maintain bone density, which menopause can otherwise be hard on.

BE GENTLE WITH YOURSELF

That said, the symptoms of menopause can also make motivation to get out the door a more formidable challenge. If you've had trouble getting consistent quality sleep and your runs are suffering as a result, don't be afraid to reduce your mileage until you've had a chance to catch up on sleep. Rest is important.

TIPS

- Worried about intermittent break-through bleeding? Wear a reusable menstrual cup on training runs or races to avoid unwanted leaks.

- Hydrate well throughout the day to stave off dehydration and electro-lyte loss caused by hot flashes and night sweats.

- Invest in a bandana or "cool wrap"—an accessory you can dampen and wear around your neck or forehead during or after a run to help keep you cool.

- Wear compression gear to pro-mote healthy blood circulation.

WEIGHT MANAGEMENT

You may find you need to adjust your diet to avoid the natural weight gain that many women experience during menopause. Consult your doctor, but many women become less tolerant of carbohydrates during menopause—so even during runs, you may find you have less of a need for sugary gels or energy bars.

THE BOTTOM LINE

Above all, treasure the fact that you are a runner! During menopause—as with all other phases of your life—just remember that a good run can do wonders to promote good health, improve your sleep quality, and boost your mood.

TAKE IT TO THE NEXT LEVEL

Connect with other women by finding a local women's trail running group, attending a group run, participating in an online forum or social media group, or treating yourself to a women's trail running retreat. If there isn't a group near you, be the instigator! Start your own group run. Invite someone who's never been trail running before and show her why you love the trails.

CHAPTER 11

TRY A RACE

Trail running is a great activity all by itself—for your body, your mind, and your soul. A lot of trail runners, though, like to take it to the next level by entering a race and getting competitive with themselves and others.

Are you one of those people? There are a lot of reasons to take part in a trail race:

- You want to improve your trail running, and having a challenge like a trail race helps make that happen.

- You're looking for an excuse to travel to a new place.

- You're competitive with yourself and against others.

- Having an objective to strive toward helps get you out the door when your motivation is flagging. You can't kick the ball down the road when there's a date fixed on the calendar!

Want to give it a try? Great! At the very least, you'll finish the day tired, happy, and with a fresh "finisher" shirt and a medal around your neck. By taking on a robust challenge complete with big ups and downs, topographically and emotionally, you'll probably also have an epic experience. And spending several hours running in a beautiful locale may inspire you to get more immersed in trail running.

This chapter lays out our tips for "toeing the line" and running your first trail race.

Setting Expectations

Whatever expectations you are bringing to your first trail race, our advice is this: take a deep breath and let them go. Just focus on the fun factor and the joy of running on trails.

Here's why: There's nothing quite like trail racing. During your first trail race, you'll experience moments of exhilaration, fatigue, self-doubt, and many more feelings. That's *normal*. After all, your first trail race is an entirely new adventure!

FEELING PHONY

Most new trail racers—and many veteran ones—experience "imposter syndrome." That's when you wonder what the hell you're doing standing at the starting line of a race with so many runners who seem to be faster, better equipped, or more seasoned than you. Don't worry—that feeling is not uncommon. You have a right to be there!

If you've run in road races, it's important to know that road racing doesn't have much in common with trail racing. First, expect your time for any given race distance to be much slower—no matter if it's a 5 km race, a 10 km race, a marathon, or any other distance. Our advice is to ignore your pace and run at a comfortable speed. But also understand that you might have to run up and down a big hill (or several hills!) early in the race, and that could spike your heart rate considerably, make you feel out of breath, and change how you feel during the rest of the race. For your first race, make finishing your primary goal. Once you cross the line, you'll gain confidence and inspiration and your foray into trail racing will be—literally—off and running.

If you let go of your expectations before you start your first trail race, you're going to have a happier experience. That means more fun, and more fun means more trail races in your future. Don't believe us? Consider the case of Stevie Kremer from Crested Butte, Colorado. She finished DFL in her first trail race—that's "dead f—ing last." But she had fun and so she kept running—and she went on to become one of the world's best trail runners.

LET GO OF YOUR EXPECTATIONS!

HAPPINESS = REALITY – EXPECTATIONS

Picking a Race

EASY ON THE DISTANCE

For your first race, the only win you need to worry about notching on your belt is ensuring that you have a good experience. Pick a distance that you have run before. You'll have plenty of new experiences during your first trail race—the challenge of a new distance shouldn't be one of them. Go easy on yourself. If your favorite distance is 10 km, run a 10 km trail race, not a 20 km one. Here's a tip about picking your distance: You're likely to run faster and harder than usual. It's just human nature when you're surrounded by a pack of eager trail runners. That means the second half of the race is going to be harder than you expect—another reason to err on the shorter side.

CHECK THE VERT

When you're looking at options for your first trail race, check online to find out how hilly the course is—the amount of vertical gain and loss, or "vert" in trail running jargon, over the course.

The amount of vert in a trail race makes a huge difference. Consider this: There's a 10 km trail race in Susa, Italy, that climbs 10,000 feet! The winning time to cover those 6 miles that go up, up, up? 1:58:53. By comparison, a middle-of-the-pack trail runner might take about an hour to complete a typical, much flatter 10 km course.

TERRAIN

Two trail races can have exactly the same distance and vertical, but be very different! The reason is that the terrain for each one is unique. Is the trail smooth and runnable, or is it filled with boulders, roots, and other technical challenges? Our advice? As best as possible, mimic the conditions of the trails you train on. That will also help you estimate your finishing time in the race and prepare you for what you'll encounter on race day. How can you figure out what the terrain is like? The race's website should help. And if the finishing times for the distance seem slow and the amount of vert doesn't seem to explain it, the answer probably has something to do with the terrain!

10 KM

1:58:53

10 KM

1:00:00

Getting to Race Day

  As race day approaches, take some specific steps to prepare, including deciding what gear you will wear and bring, planning to arrive early, and studying the race course ahead of time.

PRE-RACE TIPS

GET THE GEAR

Like road races, trail races typically have aid stations where you can re-hydrate and refuel with a variety of snacks and drinks. But often, depending on the race distance and course, you'll likely want to carry some kind of pack or vest, hydration device, and energy food or gels, too. There might even be a required gear list—check the race's website for details. You should consider carrying a lightweight wind- and water-resistant jacket or lightweight gloves, even if they're not mandatory. And whatever pack or vest you choose, practice running with it so you can get used to it before race day.

GET A HELPER

Race day can be complicated and confusing. Between figuring out how to get to the race, where to pick up your bib, finding the starting line, and getting to the course briefing, stress can add up. Bring along someone to whom you can delegate a few tasks, so you can stay calm and be ready to run when the big moment finally comes.

ARRIVE EARLY

Allow yourself extra time, removing that pressure from the list of items that might stress you out as you work your way through your pre-race to-do list. If all goes smoothly, this tactic can also help you find good parking and a more desirable spot in the porta-potty queue.

GET TO KNOW THE COURSE PROFILE

Study the course profile on the race website so you're not surprised by gnarly climbs or long downhills. Do your best to commit it to memory. Knowing where the big challenges lie will keep your morale up when they do come. If you're worried about being forgetful, take an indelible marker and draw the race profile on your arm!

REVIEW THE FINISH

Take some time to walk the final few hundred yards or even the last half mile or so of the race. You'll be running this part when you're most tired. Are there confusing turns? Does the race merge with other race distances? Take a look around when your brain is calm and fresh!

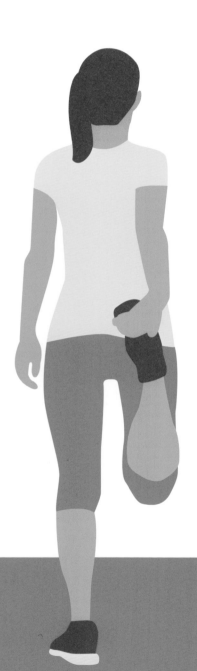

SEED YOURSELF TO SUIT YOURSELF

As you take your place amid the other racers on the starting line, consider where you want to be in the pack. From looking at the past results for the race, and perhaps having a general idea of your finish time, you might have a sense of where in the pack you are likely to finish. That's a good place to be if you don't want to be passed by faster runners. Or you might be a trail runner who gets energized by starting slower and zipping past others over the course of the race . . . in that case, start farther back than you expect to finish.

DON'T FORGET TO WARM UP

A trail race is still a trail run, and warming up is just as important—and perhaps more important, since you're likely to start fast. It's easy to get injured in a race if you start out hard on tight, cold muscles!

CONGRATULATE YOURSELF

Here's the most important fact about your race: You. Are. There. Being at the start line of a trail race means you've made a commitment to challenge yourself and push your boundaries. Plus, you've already overcome a lot: avoiding or healing from injuries, finding time to train, and balancing work, family life, and recreation. Well done!

TRAIL VEST GEAR CHECKLIST

- Energy food, electrolyte tabs, 500 mL or more of water
- Map of race course and aid stations
- First-aid items and personal medications
- Sunscreen and anti-chafing lubricant
- If it's a longer race: rain shell, extra socks, synthetic layers, hat and gloves for potential cold, headlamp and batteries

It's Race Day!

TIPS FOR WHEN YOU'RE OUT ON THE COURSE

GOING THE DISTANCE

The announced race distances are not always exact—a 5 km trail race could be a half kilometer longer, and an ultra-distance race might be several miles shorter or longer. Sometimes this is the result of an error, but often it's the result of measurement differences between your GPS device and the one used by the race organization. Give the race director a break, and don't complain about small discrepancies between an advertised race distance and what your watch is insisting is correct.

HERE'S SOMETHING
WE LOVE ABOUT TRAIL RACING

Hillary Gerardi is one of the world's top runners on tough, technical, and airy terrain. She's won races and set new course records in challenging races around the world. But she still remembers what it's like to be the newbie at a trail race. Here's one of the aspects of trail racing she loves most:

"One of the really cool things about trail racing is that you get so many people of different levels all in the same place and on the same start line. Think about it. If you're a skier, cyclist, basketball, tennis, or soccer player, you never get near the pros. If you sign up for a road marathon, you're never on the start line with the elites. Trail racing is incredible because the pros and the newbies are all out there doing it together on the same trails at the same time . . . and in my opinion, that's pretty awesome."

We couldn't have said it better!

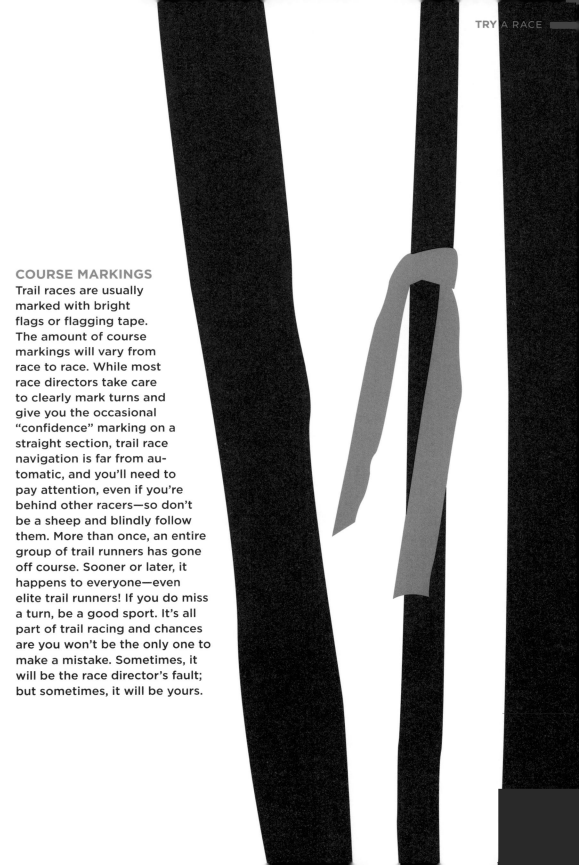

COURSE MARKINGS

Trail races are usually marked with bright flags or flagging tape. The amount of course markings will vary from race to race. While most race directors take care to clearly mark turns and give you the occasional "confidence" marking on a straight section, trail race navigation is far from automatic, and you'll need to pay attention, even if you're behind other racers—so don't be a sheep and blindly follow them. More than once, an entire group of trail runners has gone off course. Sooner or later, it happens to everyone—even elite trail runners! If you do miss a turn, be a good sport. It's all part of trail racing and chances are you won't be the only one to make a mistake. Sometimes, it will be the race director's fault; but sometimes, it will be yours.

PACING AND UPHILLS

If the race is 10 km or less, you don't need to worry too much about going out too fast—the race will be over before you know it! If the race is longer—10 miles (16 km) to marathon distance, for example—hold back and stay relaxed. Consider power-hiking up any steep hills to conserve energy. Managing your effort and recovering when the terrain gives you a chance to do so on flat and downhill sections is the key to achieving your best possible result.

HYDRATION

Be sure to start the race very well hydrated and, once the race begins, hydrate every chance you get. You don't want water sloshing around in your stomach, but staving off dehydration is important for a good result. Stick to drinks that include electrolytes, since you're also losing those when you sweat.

AID STATIONS

No matter the distance you're racing, there's likely to be at least one aid station along the way. Aid stations provide a cornucopia of calories, ranging from simple sugars and gels and soda to more substantial food like chips, pretzels, cookies, or even sandwiches, soups, pasta, and burritos. Aid stations also work to break up the race into manageable chunks, and they provide a place for your crew, family, and supporters to meet you. Check on the rules, though, as some races may not allow spectator or crew access to all aid stations.

ENERGY

If you need calories, keep it simple—gels if you don't mind them or just the liquid calories available through many soft drinks. Generally, you only need to replenish calories if you're running 90 minutes or longer. That's going to be fairly rare for shorter races, but quite normal for distances of 10 miles (16 km) or more. For your first trail race, you're unlikely to be out all day, so you don't have to eat early, or eat a lot. Besides, the harder effort of a relatively short race means your stomach is more likely to get upset.

VOLUNTEERS

Aid stations are usually staffed by volunteers. Be sure to smile and thank them for being there to serve you—and make a plan to volunteer at a race. You'll be doing your part to support trail running, and you'll have a lot of fun, too! And if a volunteer gives you a cup of Sprite instead of water? Well, be a good sport!

WHAT YOU GOT?

Check your race's website ahead of time to see what food and drink they'll have at the aid stations. If you can't stomach Gatorade or Coca-Cola, for instance, then plan ahead and have your crew meet you with your drink of choice at an aid station.

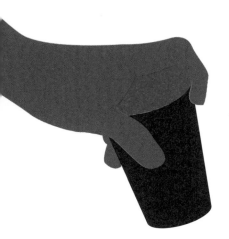

100-PROOF AID STATION

One of the most famous aid stations is Kroger's Canteen, which is at 13,000-foot-high (3962 m) Virginius Pass along the course of Colorado's Hardrock 100. In addition to the usual aid station fare, this one offers tequila and mescal to passing runners!

After the Race

CONGRATULATE YOURSELF AGAIN

Whatever the outcome, take a moment to remind yourself that you just tackled your first trail race. Congratulations! That's a huge accomplishment! And if it didn't go as you had hoped? Remember Stevie Kremer's story. (See page 181.) There's always another race, when you're ready.

POST-RACE BASH

A lot of trail races have great post-race parties. Take advantage of your post-race high, courtesy of the endorphins flowing through your brain. Grab a beer and share your race war stories with friends new and old.

TAKE CARE OF YOUR BODY

You just finished a physically and mentally challenging event. Take a few minutes to refuel with a recovery drink or snack that includes protein to heal muscles and carbohydrates to replace lost reserves. Drink plenty, which will help eliminate waste and lactic acid. Scan yourself for anything that needs attention, from blisters to Instagram-worthy cuts and bruises. Stretch anything that feels like it needs it—hamstrings, glutes, calves, hips—and if it's available, grab a free massage, too.

RECOVER

In the days after your race, give your body time to recover. The time you need will be dictated by how hard the race was for your body—and that's a function of the course and how well trained you were when you started. You're bound to feel sore, fatigued, and maybe even in pain. Stretching, such as gentle yoga, will help the recovery process. Keep hydrating, eat healthy foods, and pay attention to cravings—that's your body's way of telling you what it needs.

GET BACK TO IT!

Recovery can take anywhere from a few days to several weeks. When your body feels ready for another run, start gently, and when in doubt, err on the side of rest. Lay off getting back to running right away by prioritizing other activities like hiking, swimming, or bicycling.

Epic Trail Races around the World

Not every trail race is a 10 km run through your local forest! There are plenty of dramatic trail races around the world. Here's a look at some of the crazier ones—whether ultra-long, super steep, or wildly technical.

HARDROCK 100

 Location: Silverton, Colorado, USA

Distance and Vert: 100 miles / 161 km and 33,050 ft / 10,074 m ascent and descent

\# Number of Runners: 145

What Makes It Special: This 100-mile race through the rugged San Juan Mountains of Colorado is so popular that 1500 runners enter an annual lottery for fewer than 150 spots. The legendary mining history, warm spirit, and stunning alpine vistas make this one of the world's best-known races. Finishers aren't done until they kiss a large painted rock!

MARATHON DES SABLES

Location: Ouarzazate, Morocco

Distance and Vert: 156 miles / 250 km and 8038 ft / 2450 m ascent, 8628 ft / 2630 m descent

\# Number of Runners: 1300

What Makes It Special: Imagine running six back-to-back marathons over the "sables," or sands, of the Sahara desert! This is a stage race that takes place over seven days. The longest day is 91 km (57 miles). Water and tents are provided, but participants have to carry their own food and clothing. There are sixty medical staff working during the race, which dates back to 1986.

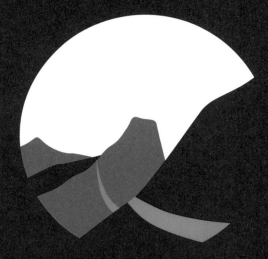

WORLD'S FASTEST VERTICAL KILOMETER

Location: Fully, Switzerland
Distance and Vert: 1.2 miles / 1.9 km and 3280 ft / 1000 m ascent
\# Number of Runners: **600**

What Makes It Special: **Using an old funicular track with a grade of 52 percent, this is one of the world's fastest vertical kilometer courses. Philip Goetsch set the world record here in 2017 with a time of 28:53—that's climbing uphill at a rate of 6814 feet (2077 m) an hour! The Fully VK is so steep that runners use poles for balance and helmets are required.**

MOUNT MARATHON

Location: Seward, Alaska, USA
Distance and Vert: 3.1 miles / 5 km and 3022 ft / 921 m ascent and descent
\# Number of Runners: **700**

What Makes It Special: **For more than a century, the residents of Seward have lined the streets each July 4 for this unique and festive race, which started as a bar bet. The treacherously steep scramble up and down Mount Marathon is legendary in its difficulty, with runners regularly bruised, bloodied, and even hospitalized.**

TOR DES GÉANTS

Location: Courmayeur, Italy

Distance and Vert: 205 miles / 330 km and; 78,740 ft / 24,000 m ascent and descent

\# **Number of Runners:** 800

What Makes It Special: A continuous, multiday race through the northern Italian Alps, the "Tour of the Giants" has a rugged verticality that tests trail runners, climbing the equivalent of 15 to 20 Empire State Buildings each day. Hallucinations are common as sleep-deprived participants push ever onward. Half of the starters drop or don't make the 150-hour time limit.

MONTE ROSA SKYMARATHON

Location: Alagna Valsesia, Italy

Distance and Vert: 21.7 miles / 35 km and 11,483 ft / 3500 m ascent and descent

\# **Number of Runners:** 400

What Makes It Special: One of the earliest races in the highly technical niche of Skyrunning, the race climbs to the Margherita hut—the highest refuge in the Alps at 14,941 feet (4554 m—then runners sprint back down to the village of Alagna Valsesia. Since participants are on glaciers for much of the race, they are required to bring technical mountaineering gear.

ULTRA-TRAIL DU MONT-BLANC

Location: Chamonix, France
Distance and Vert: 106 miles / 171 km and 32,940 ft / 10,040 m ascent and descent
 # Number of Runners: 2,300

What Makes It Special: Following the Tour du Mont Blanc hiking trail and passing through France, Italy, and Switzerland, UTMB is the world's most famous ultra-distance trail race. The high-energy atmosphere and support of thousands of volunteers is unrivaled.

TENZING HILLARY EVEREST MARATHON

Location: Everest Base Camp, Nepal
Distance and Vert: 26.2 miles / 42 km and 2982 ft / 909 m ascent, 8917 ft / 2718 m descent
 # Number of Runners: 250

What Makes It Special: This race celebrates the first ascent of Mount Everest by Sir Edmund Hillary and Tenzing Norgay in 1953 and is one of the world's highest trail races, starting at an elevation of 17,572 feet (5356 m) next to the Khumbu Icefall at Everest Base Camp.

THE JUNGLE ULTRA

Location: Manu National Park, Peru
Distance and Vert: 143 miles / 230 km and 9000 ft / 2743 m m ascent, 10,500 ft / 3200 m descent
 # Number of Runners: 50

What Makes It Special: With 100 percent humidity, hot temperatures, seventy river crossings, and a route wending through thick rainforests, this is probably one of the world's most challenging ultra-distance races. Not only must runners contend with slippery mud, thick vegetation, and poisonous snakes and spiders, they also have to be self-sufficient through the five race stages, carrying their own sleeping bag and hammock.

THE SPINE

Location: Edale, England
Distance and Vert: 268 miles / 431 km and 43,733 ft / 13,330 m ascent and descent
 # Number of Runners: 120

What Makes It Special: That this race was devised by Arctic expedition guides is no surprise—it's held in January, which ensures the worst weather possible. A nonstop race along the Pennine Way hiking trail, the course follows the high "spine" of the United Kingdom, from the Peak District to the Scottish border. Snow, gale-force winds, and torrential rain are common.

TAKE IT TO THE NEXT LEVEL

Tempted by another trail race? Great! Most runners are inspired to explore trail racing after their first experience. Having a race on the calendar is a good way to maintain fitness and help you get out the door. Explore new race challenges, like races with more vertical, different terrain, or that introduce you to a new area. Build up distance and vertical slowly in your training to minimize your risk of injury. And always remember to have fun: that'll keep you coming back for more, and will help make trail running a lifetime activity. Just be careful—before you know it, you'll need room at home for race memorabilia like finisher medals, shirts, and race bibs!

CHAPTER 12

RESPECTING THE ENVIRONMENT AND OTHER TRAIL USERS

As trail runners, we are continually immersing ourselves in the natural world, no matter if it's a remote trail in a national park or the trail at the edge of our neighborhood. Our interactions with both the environment and other visitors have a lot to do with the kind of experience we have and what we leave behind for those who come after us. As stewards of a growing sport, trail runners should strive to make a good impression, not only because it's the right thing to do, but also so that we can be assured access to trails in the years ahead. There are others who benefit, too—notably the animals and plants who call public and private lands home. When we run on trails, we're visiting their homes. Being a good guest makes their lives easier, too.

RESPECTING THE ENVIRONMENT

Respecting the environment can be trickier than it sounds. It's more than just a matter of packing out your trash. It requires planning ahead, preparing, and solid on-the-ground skills. The suggestions that follow will help you take care of the environment while also taking you one step closer to a great day on the trails.

Respect the Environment When You Plan Your Run

HOW AM I GETTING THERE?
The transportation choice we make has an impact on the trails we run. Many trailheads have limited capacity, so carpooling can reduce crowding and make life easier for land managers. Carpooling and using public transportation also reduce your carbon footprint and pollution. Keeping your car parked when you can will reduce the impact on our trails. Want to double the challenge and earn even more bragging rights? If your trailhead isn't too far away, why not bike there?

WATCH THE WET
In many areas, trails are dry and ready much of the year to handle the pounding that will come from visitors. But not always. In winter, skiing and snowshoeing can create a packed, icy ridge down the middle of the trail, forcing trail runners off the trail when the snow starts to melt. The shoulder seasons of spring and fall, when soils are saturated with water, are when trails are most vulnerable to damage. In fact, in some regions, the trails are so fragile that land managers will temporarily close them. Try to trail run where trails are driest. When trails are wet, switch gears and use "hardened" surfaces like rail trails or multiuse trails that are either paved or graveled.

SKIP THE SNOW AND MUD
Looking out your window, and seeing blue skies and dry, bare ground? Conditions may be dramatically different on a trail a few hours later, a few thousand feet higher, or with a different orientation. A trail that's north-facing and higher in elevation will hold snow, mud, and moisture longer than one that's lower and exposed to full sun. South- and west-facing slopes are often the driest. Avoiding sections of trail with snow and mud will help keep you on the trail, reducing erosion and other impacts. Help yourself and the trail by picking options that are more likely to be snow- and mud-free. Usually, that means lower-elevation, south-facing trails.

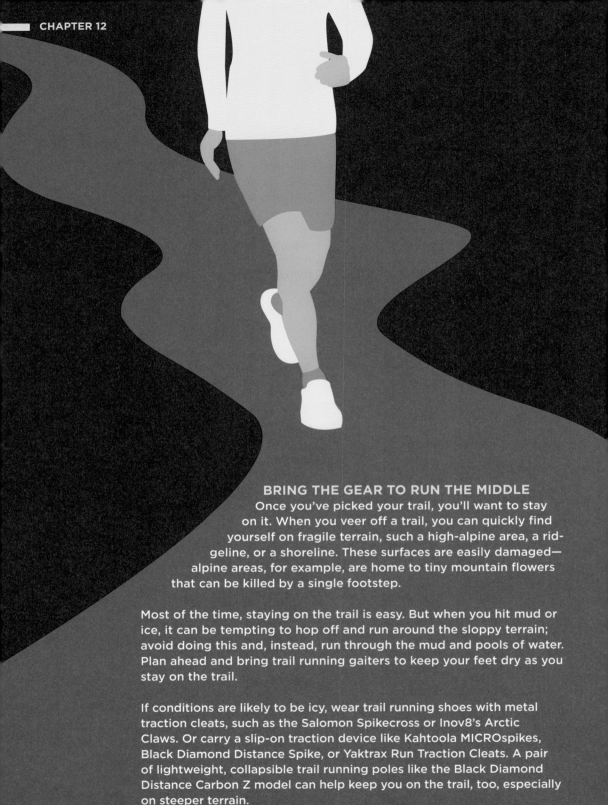

BRING THE GEAR TO RUN THE MIDDLE

Once you've picked your trail, you'll want to stay on it. When you veer off a trail, you can quickly find yourself on fragile terrain, such a high-alpine area, a ridgeline, or a shoreline. These surfaces are easily damaged—alpine areas, for example, are home to tiny mountain flowers that can be killed by a single footstep.

Most of the time, staying on the trail is easy. But when you hit mud or ice, it can be tempting to hop off and run around the sloppy terrain; avoid doing this and, instead, run through the mud and pools of water. Plan ahead and bring trail running gaiters to keep your feet dry as you stay on the trail.

If conditions are likely to be icy, wear trail running shoes with metal traction cleats, such as the Salomon Spikecross or Inov8's Arctic Claws. Or carry a slip-on traction device like Kahtoola MICROspikes, Black Diamond Distance Spike, or Yaktrax Run Traction Cleats. A pair of lightweight, collapsible trail running poles like the Black Diamond Distance Carbon Z model can help keep you on the trail, too, especially on steeper terrain.

CONSIDER A LEASH AND POOP BAGS

Off-leash dogs can cause their own environmental damage, including trampling off-trail terrain, widening trails, and scaring or chasing wildlife. Consider buying a trail running–specific leash for your dog, which retracts into the collar when not in use.

When your dog poops in the woods, it's not the same as a wild animal's poop. Rich in nitrogen and phosphorus because of a dog's diet, dog poop—multiplied by the hundreds or thousands of dogs a year that travel along some trails—can alter sensitive ecosystems. So consider bringing along poop bags for your dog when you run. And always check with the land manager first—dogs are not allowed on trails in many national parks, for example.

KNOW BEFORE YOU GO

When making plans for a more remote, adventurous trail run, try to get an update on trail conditions before you go. That might mean checking a website or social media channel of the US Forest Service, Bureau of Land Management, National Park Service, or a state or local park agency. You might also just pick up the phone and call. Most offices have a backcountry specialist who more often than not is someone who loves to be out on the trails. The right contact can provide a wealth of information regarding trail closures, recent conditions, and other on-the-ground info.

Respect the Environment on the Trail

Ready to run? Great! On the trail, there are plenty of steps you can take to help take care of the land. In doing so, you'll also be setting a great example for others, and helping to create an ethic of stewardship that will preserve the experience for future visitors. Keep these points in mind as you leave the trailhead behind.

USE THE TRAIL WORK

This is where the rubber hits the ground—literally. Staying on the trail is about more than not getting lost. When we stay on designated routes, we're using structures like rock steps, wood or rock staircases, and bog bridges. One of the goals of trail work is to keep us on the path so we don't widen the trail, causing damage. Land managers "harden" the surface of the trail so it can handle a lot of use.

Trails are built to gently slope across the "fall line"—the direct line that water would take down a hill—to minimize erosion. That's why cutting switchbacks is bad news. When we go straight up the fall line, we create an indentation water can use to flow downhill, which leads to erosion.

Keep your eyes open for trail structures the next time you're out. They may be hard to find—the best trail work is blended into the environment so as not to be obtrusive. Better yet, sign up for a trail work party so you can learn firsthand about the work that goes into maintaining a trail.

GOT TO GET OFF?
USE DURABLE SURFACES

Sometimes it's unavoidable. You have to step off the trail—when nature calls, or for that cool photo you simply have to snag for Instagram. When you do, stay on durable surfaces, which usually means rocks, sand, or gravel. During spring and fall, snow and ice are great surfaces to travel on, since they protect vulnerable plants and soils. Do the "rock hop," and protect fragile landscapes.

HOW TO GO ON THE TRAIL

Poop happens! And when it's during a trail run, it's usually no big deal. Get at least 200 feet, or about 60 meters, off the trail, for the sake of other users and for your own privacy. (For most of us, that's about 90 steps.)

Use a stick, trail running pole, or your shoe heel to dig into the topsoil, but not below it—6-8 inches (15–20 cm) is ideal. Don't go too deep—the top layer of soil is where microbes will break down your waste. If you have toilet paper with you, pack it out with you in a separate plastic bag. If you don't have TP, or if you're game to be a little adventurous, use leaves instead—just be careful not to use poison ivy or other plants with leaves that will have you itching wildly later!

Pooping into a hole avoids the "fecal plume" that results from aboveground waste washing away when it rains. In addition to the smell that results, the microorganisms in waste can pollute groundwater and make both animals and people sick.

It's more fun to poop when you can read this book at the same time! Avoid the hassle and plan your poops. Caffeinate as soon as you get up in the morning. (Good news: this is your excuse for a second cup of high-test!) If it doesn't happen on your home throne, use a toilet en route to your run.

LEAVE WHAT YOU FIND

Trail running past old mines, logging camps, or other historical locations is pretty cool. Artifacts from another era remind us of our rich human history. So preserve that experience for others and don't disturb them. The same goes for natural discoveries, like interesting rocks. Leave them so others can have the same great experience. Take photos instead. (Besides, do you really want to carry that rock in your trail running vest pocket for half the day?) Leave nature as it is and skip building piles of rocks, called cairns. When you arrange natural objects, you're creating another human impact. The existing cairns that mark the trail above tree line were built by trail crews in strategic locations. Building your own may cause someone to lose their way on a low-visibility day.

RESPECT WILDLIFE

As trail runners, it's inevitable that we'll surprise wildlife. That has consequences for your safety (see Chapter 6). But it also has implications for the animals, who perceive you as a potential threat and may have a stressful reaction to your presence. For their sake, give them a lot of breathing room, and restrain your dog, which may be perceived as a predator. Remember: We're the visitors. How would you feel if a trail runner suddenly ran through your living room?

SKIP THE POLE DANCE

Think twice before pulling out your running poles in areas with muddy or thin soils. Poles add extra impact. Research scientists have found that carbide-tipped hiking and trail running poles can cause significant damage to the soil adjacent to a trail. If you rely on your poles, consider using the rubber or plastic tips that are usually provided with them.

RACE HERE, NOT THERE

Trail running is a remarkably low-impact activity, especially when you run thoughtfully. Trail races, however, are one activity where our community can have a notable impact on the land and the experience of others.

Public land managers have to accomodate a wide range of uses—everything from mining to logging to hunting, climbing, mountain biking, snowmobiling, ATV use, and, of course, trail running.

Some of those lands have management goals that conflict with events like trail races. Very fragile environments, such as alpine areas, are examples of places where allowing large numbers of users to converge conflicts with other priorities—in this case, protecting a natural resource.

Designated wilderness areas are a well-known example. In the US, the 1964 Wilderness Act describes wilderness areas as having "outstanding opportunities for solitude or a primitive and unconfined type of recreation." In other words, solitude is a goal for the managers. As runners, we get to run all day and see just a few other folks.

As an alternative to races, which bring a lot of people together at one time, the Fastest Known Time (FKT) movement has developed. FKTs allow trail runners to run a route on their own, at their own pace and on their own time, while recording it with a GPS device—and then others can try to do the same route faster. To find an FKT near you, see FastestKnownTime.com.

Know Your Trail Etiquette

 When you're trail running, you'll encounter other users such as climbers, backcountry skiers, hikers, and hunters. Respecting their experience entails more than not inducing a heart attack as you cruise past at warp speed. There's more to trail etiquette than meets the eye! Here are our tips.

ACT LIKE YOU'RE IN CATHEDRAL

The late wilderness advocate Edward Abbey asked us to imagine that we're in a cathedral when we're in the woods—and there are some things you just don't do in a cathedral, such as carving your name somewhere or yelling. (Don't worry, you're encouraged to make some noise when you're in grizzly bear country!) The woods are special, in part because it's so peaceful. Before you yell across a ridgeline, or put a friend on speaker phone, ask yourself, "Would I do that in a cathedral?"

OKAY, BUT MAKE A LITTLE NOISE

Trail runners can come up quickly on others, who are often moving at a very different speed. Slow down when you're approaching, and let the folks in front of you know you are closing in. Besides, it might save you from having to start CPR! Usually, our conversations give us away as we approach other trail users, but if you're going solo, make a little noise and politely alert them that you'd like to pass.

KEEP IT CELL-FREE

Think before you whip out your cell phone. Is your call absolutely necessary? Most folks on trails are there to escape from the noise and hyperactivity of our busy lives, of which cell phones are a powerful symbol. Time your trip so you're not having to make calls. If a call is truly urgent, step off the trail and out of earshot. If you are bringing a phone, turn the ringer off. And when you leave the trailhead, get in the habit of putting your phone into airplane mode. In addition to not ringing and beeping when you're trying to chill, your phone will retain extra battery power in case you need it for calling a rescue, navigating, or taking photos when Kilian Jornet runs by!

TAKE IT TO THE NEXT LEVEL

The Leave No Trace Center for Outdoor Ethics is an international nonprofit that teaches everyone from horse packers to hikers to trail runners how to reduce their impact in the backcountry. Consider taking one of their classes. If a Leave No Trace (LNT) program isn't available near you, review their seven principles online at LNT.org, or check to see if any similar programs are available in your area.

CLEAN UP AFTER YOURSELF—AND OTHERS

Stopping for a snack? Take a glance to make sure everything's tidy. The old adage of "Pack it in, pack it out" is as true today as it was fifty years ago. Bring a plastic bag for microtrash, such as empty gel packets and energy bar wrappers. Having it accessible will make it easier for you to deal with trash while you're on the go.

GET SMALL

Studies show that the size of your group directly impacts the perceived experience of others. Breaking a large group of, say, ten, into three smaller groups results in a perception of fewer people on the part of those you meet. However, even these smaller groups tend to meet up again at fragile areas like alpine summits. So consider keeping your group small to begin with.

Sometimes it's even the law. Land managers often have group size regulations, particularly in wilderness areas and national parks. Check before you go!

IT'S OUR RESPONSIBILITY

As trail runners, we've made a conscious decision to veer off the roads. One common reason is that we're seeking a quieter, wilder experience. We're fortunate to have that opportunity. With it comes responsibility—to ourselves, to the land, to others. Share your good habits, spreading the ethic of steward-ship to your fellow trail runners. The sport of trail running, wild places, and the experience of others will all benefit.

CHAPTER 13

WHEN 26.2 MILES ISN'T ENOUGH: RUNNING AND RACING ULTRA DISTANCES

Why Run Ultra Distances, Anyway?

Run long over the course of a day—or sometimes even several consecutive days and nights—and you'll be pushing your mind and body into uncharted territory. There are big challenges, but also great rewards, to going beyond the marathon distance. Here are some of the reasons you might want to consider running more than 26.2 miles (42 km).

WHEN YOU RUN ULTRAS, YOU'LL GET TO . . .

- Build extraordinary endurance and all-around fitness.

- Explore wild and remote places up close that you can't reach on shorter runs.

- Learn about being self-sufficient.

- Know yourself better—your limits, as well as your ability to tackle tough challenges.

- Have a lot of contemplative quiet time to yourself, something a lot of us are missing in today's busy society. Some long-distance trail runners even say ultrarunning has qualities similar to meditation.

- Connect with a unique community of inspiring, ambitious, and supportive individuals.

- Experience aspects of the natural world we often miss—like sunrises, sunsets, and being outside at night.

- Brag when your coworkers ask you, incredulously, "Tell me again how far you ran this weekend?"

WHAT'S THE BIG DEAL ABOUT BIG DISTANCES?

Running longer than a 26.2-mile (42 km) marathon officially launches you into ultramarathon territory. Ultra trail running has been growing for two decades, and in recent years it has exploded in popularity. For good reason, too! Trail running very long distances rewards both the body and the spirit. But going far on your feet also presents unique challenges. If you're curious about racing an ultra, the common distances include 50 km (31 miles), 50 miles (80 km), 100 km (62 miles), 100 miles (161 km), and, in recent years, even 200 miles (322 km)!

Still curious? Let's take a look at what happens when you run a marathon . . . and then keep going.

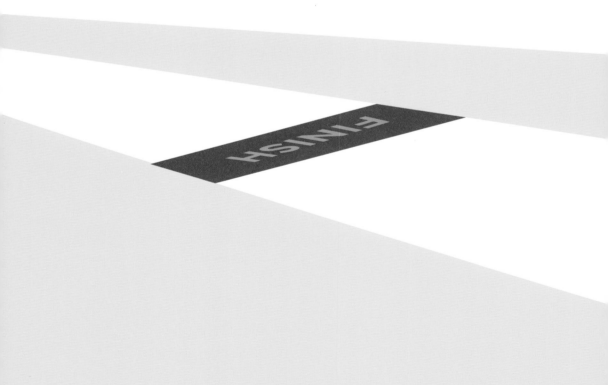

Prepping for Stepping Past 26.2 Miles

 Trail running long distances presents some unique challenges that are different from going out on your local trails for an hour or two. Here are a few things to consider if you'd like to trail run 30, 40, 50, or 200 miles at a time.

FIRST, FIND THE TIME

To prepare to run long distances, you're going to need to make space for long training runs. Do you have big chunks of time available for training in your life?

SLOW DOWN

Because you'll be trail running for so much more time, you're going to be moving more slowly than you have in the past. In fact, you'll likely be fast-hiking long sections, especially when going up hills. Adjust your expectations!

CAN YOU STOMACH IT?

Your stomach might get finicky after hours of running. That can become a serious challenge, because one of the important aspects of ultrarunning is the ability to continually fuel by consuming calories. Do you know what you can stomach after a dozen hours of slow running? You'll need to experiment and find out what works for you. You should plan to snack steadily throughout the run, so you don't bonk. Getting fats and protein into your body is important to power you through a long day.

MORE WATER, PLEASE

Going the distance means you're going to need to replace a lot of fluids—far more than the liter or two you can carry in your trail running vest. You'll need to find a route that has plenty of potable water options, or water you can treat with a filter. Those options might include huts, parks with drinking fountains, towns with places to buy water, and fast-flowing streams.

LIGHT IT UP

Choosing the right headlamp can be tricky. It's not just about being able to see the ground at night, it's also about making sure it fits well on your head. You should be able to adjust the strap quickly, and your headlamp should fit comfortably with any hats, caps, and jacket hoods you like to wear. Get comfortable with your headlamp and its settings, and be able to quickly change batteries, too!

KNOW YOUR NIGHT MOVES

Running long distances means you'll almost certainly be spending time running at night, either early in the morning or after sunset . . . or both. Practice running at night for an hour or two, so you get used to the feel. Try it when you're tired, too, so you really know what to expect!

GEAR UP

To take care of yourself when you're outside for longer periods of time, you'll need to carry more clothing and gear, and you might need a larger trail running pack to hold it all! See our gear list on page 227.

WATCH THE CHAFE

More running means little irritations have plenty of time to turn into big ones. Chafing and blisters will appear in the usual places, and in a few that you've never considered! (Who'd have thought a bra strap or the liner of a pair of running shorts could draw blood?) If you're unsure how your shoes will treat your feet, have a second pair of shoes and socks ready to go somewhere along your route.

FIND A FRIEND

Hours spent on the trail will go by faster with a friend or two at your side. Plus, you'll have a partner with you to endure the grind of the long miles and difficult terrain, and be there for support in case something goes wrong. Four-footed friends are great company, too—just make sure they're allowed on the trails where you're headed, and are themselves trained for the challenge!

BREAK IT DOWN

Even for experienced ultrarunners, the idea of running all day, or sometimes continuously for several days, will blow a fuse in their brains. Instead, break your adventure down into many smaller runs. Focus on a goal that's a few hours away. Then pick another, and another. Before you know it, you'll be well on your way!

SEEK SUPPORT

If you can, have a friend meet you en route. He or she can bring you food, water, and other necessary supplies—like a small carton of your favorite ice cream. It will be a great morale boost!

SET A TURNAROUND TIME

A lot can slow you down over long distances, and you might have misjudged your speed when you were doing the math on the sofa. Instead of finishing your run hours late with your headlamp battery dying, set a turnaround time for a point partway in—and stick to it. You can always come back later and try again!

GO BACK-TO-BACK

Getting fit to complete ultra-distance runs requires aerobic development, all-body strength, and the ability to run while you're fatigued. Running one long trail run and recovering the next day is not the same as running multihour runs on back-to-back days. That kind of training will simulate what it feels like to run an ultra distance. You'll also have a chance to learn how to manage both physical and mental fatigue.

SHARE YOUR PLAN

Particularly if you're headed out solo, let a trustworthy friend or two know your plans. Make sure they check in with you when you're expected back in town, too! If you plan to frequently run alone in remote areas, consider getting a satellite messenger, like a SPOT device or Garmin inReach.

PEAKS AND VALLEYS!

Despite all these tips, there will still be times when your spirits will sag and you won't quite know what to do. Here's the good news: These moments don't last forever. If you keep going, there is a good chance you'll feel much better in an hour or so. Listen to the wisdom of Kilian Jornet, one of the world's top trail runners: "The important thing is moving." Instead of dwelling on the negative, find something that's going well during your run, and focus on that.

SUGGESTED GEAR FOR ULTRARUNNING

Start with the basics—check out our list in Chapter 3—but make sure your shoes have plenty of padding and comfort. There are trail running shoes made just for running ultra distances!

- An additional layer of warm clothing, hat, and gloves (if in cold areas)

- Anti-chafing lube

- About 240 calories per hour of high-energy snacks

- Electrolyte tablets to replace salts and micronutrients lost while sweating

- Sunblock

- Cell phone, possibly with battery backup

- Headlamp with extra batteries, plus a lightweight backup headlamp

- A map or maps that include adjacent areas, in case you make a wrong turn. Download digital maps to your phone so they are available without a cell signal.

- Money, credit card, ID, health insurance card

- Simple first-aid kit, including a self-adhesive bandage

- Toilet paper. Tuck it into a small plastic bag to keep it away from sweat and rain. (See page 208 to learn how to poop in the woods.)

- A minimum of a liter of water to get you started, either in soft flask bottles, handheld bottles, or a hydration bladder

- A bigger trail running pack. With more gear to carry, your current trail running vest might not be up to the task. Consider a vest or trail running pack with a 10-to-20-liter capacity.

Ready, Set, Go: Trail Racing Ultra Distances

Our advice for running your first ultra race is simple: build up slowly. By learning about your body, your mind, and your equipment little by little, you are more likely to avoid making gargantuan mistakes.

Racing an ultramarathon comes with some inherent challenges. Here are our tips to get ready for toeing the line.

CONSIDER A COACH

If you're new to ultra racing, there's a lot to learn. And working up to long distances can take time. A trail running coach can help you bypass a lot of trial and error—and maybe an injury or two as well.

READ UP

There are plenty of good resources for tackling ultra-distance trail races. Buy a book or two. Check out the wealth of information online. A few of our favorites: irunfar.com, *Ultrarunning* magazine and its companion website, and books like *Running Your First Ultra* by Krissy Moehl, *Hal Koerner's Field Guide to Ultrarunning*, and *Training Essentials for Ultrarunning* by Jason Koop.

CONSIDER A CREW

Having a friend or two meet you at aid stations can really help when you're feeling a bit spacey. Plus, seeing their faces will make you smile and keep you upbeat. During an ultra race, that's important!

FOLLOW THE FLAGS

When you are out there racing, watch carefully for the course markings. Long routes over rough terrain may become confusing, especially if you haven't slept for a night or two or the weather suddenly gets ugly.

KNOW YOUR NEEDS

To successfully race long distances, you're going to need to know what your body needs. To move through aid stations more quickly, formulate a plan. What bottle will you fill, and with what? What will you likely eat and drink while you are there? Do you need to address blisters or apply more sunblock? What energy snacks do you need to restock in your vest? Do you have trash to unload?

CHECK THE REQUIRED GEAR LIST

Many long-distance races have a list of required gear, because you're likely to be far from help for much of the race. Check the list twice before you travel to the race. Some items might be hard to source locally once you get there.

PICK A PACER

Some trail ultramarathons allow runners to have a pacer join them for much of the race. A pacer, like any partner, can be invaluable company. The miles will fly by, and your pacer will know just the speed you need to keep up your forward progress.

15-MINUTE MILE

MAKE A FRIEND

Even if the race doesn't allow pacers, or you don't have one, you can always make a new friend. After the first hour or so, the race pack usually spreads out. At some point you might end up running with someone for a few minutes, a few hours, or much longer. Striking up a conversation when you both have some oxygen to spare can be a great morale boost. Added bonus: the ultrarunning community is not short on interesting personalities.

START SLOW

There's a saying in running: "If you want to run fast, run slow." In other words, start slowly. Statistically speaking, if you run faster in the second half of a race (a "negative split"), you're probably going to have your fastest possible race result. So start slowly and save some energy for the second half. You'll be passing tired ultrarunners left and right!

DO SOME WALKING

Ultra-distance races are all about relentless forward motion, and if that means walking, then go ahead and walk. Walking or hiking up moderate and steep inclines is usually much more efficient than trying to run. And sometimes your body just needs a time-out, even if the terrain is flat. Taking a walking break can help you recover a bit, allow you to digest any food or drinks you've just consumed, and give your mind a break.

ARRIVE PREPARED

There are no shortcuts to getting in shape and learning what you need to know to run longer than a marathon. Start with a few ultra-distance runs on your favorite trails—even on back-to-back days—before trying a race. Get comfortable with the distance and the duration before you put yourself into the grueling grind of a race setting.

When Things Go Wrong

 Despite your best efforts, things will go wrong during ultras. In fact, that's kind of the point—coping with adversity and problem-solving along the way are part of what makes getting through an ultra-distance run such an accomplishment. Because you're out there for so long, it's practically inevitable: you're going to come face-to-face with some unanticipated challenges. Here are some of the more common problems—and how to solve them.

A SUFFERING STOMACH

During long periods of exercise when blood is diverted to other organs, your stomach might start to shut down and you might have trouble digesting the calories and drinks you're consuming. If you eat too much, you might even experience some lightheadedness. (It's not yet clear why this happens, but it could be that your blood is being shunted to your gut to aid in digestion, or it could be something called "reactive hypoglycemia," which is not uncommon.)

To avoid stomach problems—or worse, diarrhea and vomiting—try to eat small amounts of food at regular intervals, while drinking appropriate amounts of water. Savory snacks are ideal, since they will help replace the salt you're losing through sweat. But the best snack is the one that you and your stomach both like!

BONKING

Bonking, or "hitting the wall," happens when the glycogen in your muscles is depleted. You might experience it in the form of physical fatigue that makes it hard to keep running, or you might start to come a bit unglued mentally, becoming stubborn and making bad decisions. The good news is that the dreaded bonk can almost always be fixed by resting a bit and eating or drinking carbohydrates. You can avoid bonking in the first place by eating and drinking regularly and not starting too fast.

BLISTERS

Do you have spots on your feet where blisters or hot spots are common? Duct tape that area in advance to avoid blisters, or lube it up before the race. If you feel a blister in the works, stop and deal with it right away by applying Compeed or 2nd Skin anti-blister cushions.

GETTING INJURED

Tripping and falling is an unfortunate part of trail running, but you can often avoid injuries if you tuck and roll before you hit the ground. If you do get hurt, take a moment to assess the situation and deal with it as best you can. Carrying self-adhesive tape can help you manage a sprain or a cut. Try to walk for a bit before you start running again. Eat and drink a little extra, too—your body will thank you. If you're seriously hurt, ask other runners for help and to alert race officials.

GOING OFF ROUTE

If happens to everyone—even elite runners like Jim Walmsley. (See page 124.) Especially toward the end of a race, consciously pay close attention to course markings. Be cautious when you're following a group of runners ahead of you. They're not always right! If you think you're lost, stop and retrace your steps to the previous marker.

STAY POSITIVE

If everything seems to be going wrong, focus on how you can make things go right. Positive self-talk can be very effective. Find something to appreciate, such as the beautiful weather, the amazing views, the fact that you've already ticked off 30 miles . . . you name it. It can be as simple as the fact that you're there, trying your best in an ultra! As time passes, you'll find you're more relaxed and focused—and you'll start to notice you're running better and having more fun.

DROP IF YOU MUST

If worse comes to worst, and it's just not your day, dropping out of a race is always okay. Go to the next race checkpoint and inform someone working for the race that you want to drop out. They might take your bib, or put an X across it with a magic marker, and they'll help you get transportation. Remember: It's only a trail race, you gave it your best try, and there'll be another chance to reach your goal. Congratulate yourself for making it as far as you did, and take time to turn any lingering disappointment into inspiration for your next race.

A Few Classic, Epic—and Downright Insane—Ultras

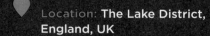

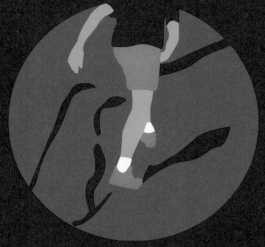

BOB GRAHAM ROUND

Location: The Lake District, England, UK

Distance: 66 miles / 106 km

This beautiful and rugged loop over 42 "fells," or hills, is a classic test of endurance for trail runners from around the world. The route is named for the local Keswick, England, guesthouse owner who first managed to complete the route in under 24 hours, in 1932. Today, running it in under 24 hours is still the goal—but you need to be fast to do that. If you're not in a rush, take a few days to run it, and stay at some inns along the way.

ULTRA-TRAIL DU MONT-BLANC

Location: Around Mont Blanc in the Western Alps, through France, Switzerland, and Italy

Distance: 106 miles / 171 km

UTMB is, hands down, the world's most famous ultra race, and the route itself has become a classic ultra-distance trail run, accomplished over two to six days. Starting and finishing in Chamonix, France, it runs through three different countries, each with its own distinct culture and welcoming mountain huts. The views and the trails are inspiring nearly every step of the way. Running it over six days is about right if you want to enjoy the sights and culture along the way. (The winners of the UTMB trail race along the same route take just under 20 hours to run around 15,777-foot (4809 m) Mont Blanc!)

NOLAN'S 14

Location: Sawatch Range, Colorado, USA

Distance: 80+ miles / 129+ km

In 1991, Fred Vance challenged Jim Nolan to see how many peaks over 14,000 feet (4267 m)—14ers—he could fit into a 100-mile (161 km) route. Nolan, who had climbed all of Colorado's 54 peaks over that height, returned a week later with what is now known as Nolan's 14, a north–south line connecting fourteen peaks in the Sawatch Range. Anyone can complete this route from Mount Massive to Mount Shavano in either direction, and you can choose your own route linking the fourteen 14ers. The goal is to go under 60 hours—but that's tough, unless you're super fit!

JOHN MUIR TRAIL

Location: Between Yosemite National Park and Whitney Portal, California, USA

Distance: 223 miles / 359 km

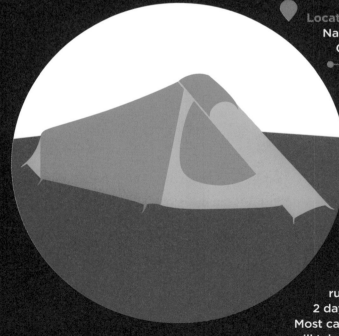

The JMT winds its way through the rugged wilderness of three national parks deep in the heart of California's Sierra Nevada. You need to be self-sufficient, carrying your own supplies and setting up food caches in advance to pick up along the way. Now we're getting into really epic territory! The fastest time, held by French runner François D'Haene, is 2 days, 19 hours, and 26 minutes. Most casual "fastpacking" trail runners will take 10–12 days.

GRAND RAID DE LA RÉUNION, DIAGONALE DES FOUS

Location: Réunion Island, Indian Ocean
Distance: 103 miles / 165 km

Known as the "Madman's Diagonal," this route traverses the tropical island of La Réunion in a diagonal line from the south to the north—from the ocean, across several highly technical climbs of over 6500 feet (1980 m), then back down to sea level. Winners of the annual race run the route in about 24 hours, but you should aim for a week if you're taking your time.

MUSTANG TRAIL

Location: Kagbeni to Jomsom, Nepal
Distance: 103 miles / 166 km

The Mustang Trail Race is an eight-day high-altitude stage race through Nepal's magical Mustang region, in the Annapurna Conservation Area. The fastest times are around 19 hours—though most runners take 30 to 50 hours. The race is organized by Trail Running Nepal, a company that supports Nepali runners. The route climbs up to a maximum of 14,100 feet (4300 m). Trail runners can explore the route on their own, too, though extensive planning, a local guide, and a permit are a must.

THE BADWATER ULTRAMARATHON

 Location: **Death Valley, California, USA**
Distance: **135 miles / 217 km**

Badwater describes itself as "The World's Toughest Footrace," and for good reason. The race starts in Death Valley, California, 279 feet (85 m) below sea level, and sends runners on paved roads across a scorching hot desert—where temperatures can reach 130°F (54°C)—to the trailhead at the base of Mount Whitney at 8360 feet (2548 m) above sea level.

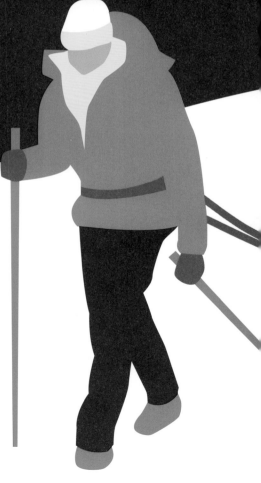

YUKON ARCTIC ULTRA

 Location: **Yukon Territory, Canada**
Distance: **100–430 miles / 161–692 km**

This event offers three grueling race distances (plus a marathon) in the cold and rugged winter conditions of the Yukon Territory, where temperatures typically range from -12°F to -25°F (-24°C to -32°C). Competitors, who can opt to go on foot, on cross-country skis, or by bike, have to pull a sled and carry all of their mandatory equipment and food. Just finishing the race is considered a win!

SELF-TRANSCENDENCE RACE

 Location: **Queens, New York, USA**
Distance: **3100 miles / 5000 km**

Created by Indian spiritual leader and meditation teacher Sri Chinmoy, this race stretches the definition of a trail race, since it circles a city block 5649 times. Some of the prizes the winners have received include a DVD and a T-shirt. The fastest time ever is 40 days, 9 hours, 6 minutes, and 21 seconds, but competitors have 52 days to complete the event!

BARKLEY MARATHONS

Location: **Wartburg, Tennessee, USA**
Distance: **100 miles / 161 km**

Consisting of five 20-mile (32 km) loops and 54,200 feet (16,520 m) of climbing, the quirky Barkley race passes through some of the most rugged off-trail terrain anywhere in the world. From its first edition in 1986 to 2019, only fifteen different runners have finished the race, which starts when race director Gary Cantrell, aka Lazarus "Laz" Lake, lights a cigarette.

TAKE IT TO THE NEXT LEVEL

Running an ultra is all about taking it next level. Start with something that feels daring but within reach. If you've never run one before, how about setting up your own informal race along a 50 km distance, without a crazy amount of vertical or technical running? Grab some friends, figure out a few impromptu aid stations along the way, and make a weekend out of it! By Monday morning, you'll have stories to tell at the office. (And we bet you'll already be figuring out your next run, too.)

CHAPTER 14

YOU CAN RUN THAT, TOO!

Trails come in all shapes and sizes. The good news is that we can run them all! Developing your trail running technique helps you become the ultimate all-terrain vehicle, confident enough to tackle anything, no matter where you land. Here's how to make it happen!

Running Steeply Up . . .

Running uphill on trails isn't easy. Fatigue, altitude, the relative steepness of an incline, and the inconsistency of stride length can make even short uphill sections feel like a long, frustrating slog on a treadmill set at its maximum incline. Fortunately, there are several ways to improve your uphill running and make it all feel much easier. Try out these tips the next time you're pushing hard uphill!

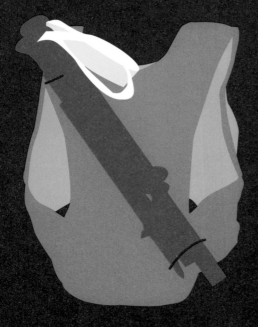

1. **IT'S OKAY TO HIKE. IN FACT, IT'S RECOMMENDED!**
   Psst, don't tell anyone! When you trail run uphill, you don't need to run. In fact, even the world's best trail runners power-hike when they are racing. Why? It's more efficient, and then you're rested and ready to run the upcoming long downhill!

2. **ADD POLES TO YOUR REPERTOIRE**
   Carbon-fiber trail running poles are a lifesaver when climbing. They engage your upper body and give a huge assist. Use a "diagonal stride," where the right pole moves forward at the same time as your left foot, and vice versa. Lightly grip the poles with your hands, letting most of the pushing take place from your wrist resting on the strap. No poles available? Alternate pushing hard on your thighs.

3. FOCUS ON FORM

Short strides will save the day. Keep your head up just enough to look at the path ahead and choose the most level stepping surfaces you can find, such as a flat rock or a dip in the ground. Try to stand tall, avoiding getting too hunched over. Use a strong, compact arm swing.

4. GET READY TO SCRAMBLE

If you need to use your hands for some scrambling, it's time to put your poles away—find the best method of securing them onto your pack beforehand. Take your time to look and feel around for the best handholds and foot placements.

5. BREATHE IN SYNC

Try to coordinate your breathing in a rhythm that matches your cadence and arm swing. Being in sync will feel better and ultimately allow you to run more efficiently.

6. STRIDE OVER THE TOP

As you approach the top of the climb, no matter the distance, stride through the summit so you can glide into the ensuing downhill.

7. WHATEVER YOU DO, DON'T LOOK UP

We're mostly serious here. Don't look up—at least not *all* the way. A big climb can be psychologically defeating. Besides, you're taking it one step at a time. Settle in, and before you know it you'll be at the top taking in a huge view.

IT'S JUST 10 KM LONG

Like going uphill? Do we have a route for you! The Triple Vertical Kilometer in the little village of Susa, Italy, rises 9970 feet (3040 m) in 6 miles (9.7 km) to reach the summit of Mount Rocciamelone at 11,608 feet (3538 m). It's so steep that a middle section of the route, called *il pratone*, reaches angles of 50 percent, at one point rising 1640 feet (500 m) in 0.6 mile (1 km)— enough to cause some trail runners to slip and start sliding downhill.

FULLY CRAZY

Races that take you up very steep routes, including vertical kilometer (VK) courses that go uphill 3280 feet (1000 m) in 3.1 miles (5 km) or less, have been gaining in popularity. One of the world's faster VK courses is in Fully, Switzerland, and it goes directly up an old funicular track, taking just 1920 meters (1.2 miles) to climb 1000 meters! World records have been set here, including the current men's record of 28:53, set by Italy's Philip Goetsch in 2017.

. . . and Running Steeply Down

1. **HEADS UP!**
   Keep your head up and scan several meters ahead, rather than just looking immediately in front of you. As you approach a switchback or are coming around a corner, look around the corner like a race car driver. This subconsciously prepares your body for what it will need to do a few steps later.

2. **TURN 'EM OVER—FAST**
   Stay light on your feet, and try for a high cadence, or turnover, in your steps. Those short, fast strides will give you more stability as gravity speeds you downhill. Although it may seem counterintuitive, get your body weight forward, allowing it to spread over the soles of your feet. How do you know if you're not leaning forward enough? If you lean back too much, your weight will be on your heels and your feet will slip forward.

3. **STRONG TO THE CORE**

Use your arms for balance, but keep your core strong. You may find your arms flailing around a bit, which can help with balance, but try to keep your core stable.

4. **DEPLOY THE POLES**

Remember those poles you had for the uphill push? They can be helpful going down, too. On very steep descents, place your poles in front of you to reduce the impact of a big step on your quads. Keep your hands out of the wrist loops to avoid injury in case you tumble.

5. **ON PLUMMETING DOWN**

If your downhill suddenly gets really, really steep, and you're freaking out . . . turn around. Face into the hillside and use your hands to climb down. Look down at your feet so that you can see where you are stepping to avoid slipping.

6. **IT'S OKAY TO FALL**

To get fast downhill, you need to challenge yourself—and the thing about challenging yourself is that sometimes you'll fail . . . and fall. That's okay. Chances are, all you'll get is a scrape that you can show off on Instagram! If you're scared about falling, try wearing lightweight cotton gloves. Some runners feel better about falling knowing they can put their hands out without getting scraped or bruised palms.

That Wasn't in the Brochure

Trail run enough, and sooner or later you'll come to a section of trail that leaves you scratching your head, wondering, "So . . . what now?!"

RIVER CROSSINGS

Fast-moving water is powerful! Slow down and consider your options.

1. **FIND THE BRAID**
   (You did look for a bridge first, right?) Divide and conquer! Crossing a big river is much easier if you can find a spot where it's divided into multiple smaller rivers.

2. **CROSS WHERE THE CONSEQUENCES ARE LOW**
   Falling into a river can lead to a lot of laughs . . . but if the river's fast and deep, or the air temperature is cold, the results can be serious. So look for a spot to cross where—if you end up in the drink—you won't go underwater, you won't kiss a rock, and you won't be swimming for your life.

3. DIP YOUR POLES

Crossing a river is a great time to use your trail running poles. When you're rock-hopping, put both poles in the water and pole-vault yourself across the gap.

4. IS IT TIME TO GET WET?

Most river crossings can be accomplished by picking the right location, using your poles, and rock-hopping across. But sometimes the river is just too wide. If that's the case, start across, using your poles and keeping your shoes on for added security. In most cases, your trail running shoes will dry quickly.

5. WHEN THE FLOW'S FAST

Flowing fast enough, a small amount of water can be very powerful. If you're crossing a river with water that comes above your knees, use caution. Loosen your vest or pack so that if it snags on a tree, you won't get caught up in the ensuing tangle. Use your poles, take small steps, and if necessary, lock arms with a friend.

6. TURN BACK

Turning back is always an option. Falling into a river can have big-time consequences. It's easy to underestimate the power of fast-moving water, which can knock you down if it's much more than knee-deep. Come back another day, when water levels are lower.

SNOWFIELDS

Snowfields can sneak up on trail runners. They are often hiding on north-facing slopes up high, late into the spring or early summer. Proceed with caution!

1. **SKIRT IT**
   Not every snowfield needs to be crossed. Go around them if you can, but beware of ending up on steeper or rockier terrain.

2. **CONSIDER THE RISKS**
   Consider the likelihood of a fall—and the result. Will it be an icy butt and a load of laughs . . . or a long tumble off an Eiger-sized cliff? If a fall is likely, but the outcome fun, go for it! If the outcome is a ride in a helicopter, maybe it's time to devise a plan B.

3. **ICY? WAIT IT OUT**
   If the snowfield is icy and the result of a fall could be serious, can you wait an hour or two? Sometimes when the sun comes around the corner, a snowfield will turn from icy ogre to playful corn snow in minutes.

4. **RECIPE: JUST ADD TRACTION**
   If you're headed for snow country, don't forget your traction! (See page 204.) Crampons for your trail running shoes are cheap insurance, plus they are light and easy to carry.

5. **STAY IN THE TRACKS**
   Ready to cross? Staying in existing tracks will help you maintain balance. Just make sure conditions haven't changed since the last person came through. If the weather has been warm, yesterday's safe step could lead to you punching through a snowbridge.

6. AND IF THERE AREN'T ANY TRACKS? KICK 'EM IN!

Looking at untrammeled ground? Face in toward the slope and then kick your toes firmly into the snow with each step, creating platforms for your feet.

7. BACK TO THE STICKS

Get those trail running poles out again—those two extra points of contact on uncertain terrain will keep you upright and smiling. Take your hands out of the wrist loops, in case you fall.

8. DON'T PUNCH THROUGH

Remember that traveling on snow is not the same thing as being on the ground. Snow is a dynamic surface that changes with factors like air temperature and humidity. Hidden surprises include snowbridges, which can form quickly as water runs under the snow. Some snowbridges can be many meters high. Listen for sounds of water and scan for visual indications you might be crossing a river.

Snow over boulder fields can be anything from fun to annoying to dangerous. Steer clear of any boulders sticking out of the snow. Their darker color absorbs heat, melting snow and creating air pockets into which you can plunge. Remember that snow is ever-changing. So don't assume that yesterday's footprints are necessarily your steps to safety!

EXPOSURE!

Sometimes, the trail gets narrow with steep sides, striking fear into your heart. Usually, that fear is a good thing—it keeps us safe. But too much fear can paralyze us. Take these steps to stay cool while tiptoeing along a perilous precipice.

1. **ASSESS THE RISK AND THE CONSEQUENCE**
   How easy is the trail? If you're unlikely to fall, that's a plus. Next, just as with the snowfield, look at the consequences. If you're going to be reaching terminal velocity, do a gut check and ask yourself if you really want to go ahead. You can always say, "Not today!" If the fall is a few feet with a safe landing, the consequences might be less severe—though even a short fall can result in an injury.

2. **SECURE IT**
   Get ready to rumble. Stop to make sure all your clothes and equipment are securely fastened. There's no tripping allowed now!

3. **WHAT'S THE RUSH?**
   When you're ready to cross, take your time. There's no rush. Watch the ground for obstacles, and if there's a cliff above to one side, look for handholds on the cliff wall.

4. **REMEMBER THOSE POLES WE JUST MENTIONED?**
   They'll be helpful here, too! (Now can you see why we like trail running poles?)

5. **BE A COOL CAT**
   Moving through exposed terrain is a mind game. Staying cool is what it's all about. Watch and focus on your breathing, and remind yourself that you are doing just fine. Focus your attention on the task at hand: look at where you're placing your feet, and hands if applicable, to help you avoid having your gaze drift over to the void. If you're with a friend and think you're going to lose your cool . . . put him or her in front and focus on the backs of his or her shoes. Don't freak out by looking to the steep sides, no matter how curious you are!

VERTIGO!

Fear of heights comes in all shapes and sizes. Sometimes it starts as a normal fear that grows into a psychological wall that feels insurmountable. Other times, it's true vertigo—a physical condition involving the inner ear that requires medical treatment. In many cases, our ability to cope with exposure gets harder with age. If you're worried about tackling an exposed trail run, speak up and let your friends know! They can help you cross that airy divide . . . or find a run that's less frightful.

TAKE IT TO THE NEXT LEVEL

Trail running is venturing into all kinds of new terrain—including steep stuff, with elite runners like Kilian Jornet and Anton Krupicka taking on runs that incorporate rock climbing levels of exposure. Want to explore that more? Take a climbing class at a local gym so you can gain confidence moving on steep terrain. Even if you never climb, the skills you learn will benefit you when the trail tilts uphill.

255

CHAPTER 15

A LIFETIME ACTIVITY

Okay, so running on trails is pretty amazing, isn't it? It's a fun way to get outdoors, get some exercise, and meander through wild places. But the real beauty of trail running is that it can be whatever you want it to be. You can run for 20 minutes on the same trail near your home every day, or you can run for hours on remote trails in far-flung mountain ranges. You can enter 5 km or 10 km trail races, or challenge yourself with a multiday ultramarathon.

Trail running can be a lifelong activity, with all kinds of benefits that accrue as you age.

Recent studies show that running is good for your knees, and it takes years off your cardiovascular age. Mentally, trail running has been shown to have all kinds of antidepressive effects, too. And let's face it, it just feels good!

The key to making trail running sustainable is finding ways to stay healthy and strong as you age, and to keep it fun. Here are some inspiring ways to make both those things happen!

Trail Running When Older

1. **ADD STRENGTH TRAINING**
    As we age, we naturally lose muscle mass. In fact, after age thirty, we lose as much as 3–5 percent per decade. That matters, because your muscle mass underlies nearly every component of your health, including strength, energy, and your ability to remain active. Adding a simple weight training program that bolsters your leg and core muscles a few times a week can halt that process.

2. **INCORPORATE BALANCE AND FLEXIBILITY TRAINING**
    Aging impacts our balance and flexibility. But as with strength training, there are many ways to slow that process. Yoga is a great way to do that. If you're apprehensive about trying yoga, you'll find an endless array of yoga videos for runners online. There are also many excellent classes for yoga novices, too.

3. **FIND A NO- OR LOW-IMPACT WAY TO TRAIN**
    On your non-running days, go easy. You can maintain fitness without hammering your body. Try mixing in some swimming, cycling, or an elliptical machine at your local gym. You'll add a cross-training component, and your body will thank you. When you do run, pick trails over roads. They're less jarring!

4. BE NICE TO YOUR BODY

In general, you're going to be less able to cut corners in your training and your rest. (Remember what we said earlier? Rest is an important part of training!) Go easy on your body. Get plenty of rest, be doubly cautious not to overtrain, and don't try to ramp up the distance too quickly.

5. DON'T COMPARE YOURSELF TO . . . YOURSELF

If you like to run the same routes or races, don't fret when your times invariably slow down a bit as the years pass. Accept it with grace and a sense of humor. Besides, it's going to happen to all of us. (And wouldn't your rather be that cool old runner who is still running with joy, instead of that irascible old-timer?)

6. REMEMBER, YOU'RE AN EXPERT NOW

All those years of trail running have given you something that would have really helped when you were younger: wisdom. That's another tool in your trail running toolbox. You'll make better decisions each day you run, and on race days. You'll run smarter races, know just where to place your feet on technical terrain, and remember to drink before you get thirsty and eat before you bonk. Remember this fact when you head out: that self-confidence will help you keep that forward motion going!

7. KEEP SHOWING UP

A big part of trail running success as you age is simply this: keep showing up. You don't need to run long. You don't need to run fast. What you need is to keep the routine going. Don't forget the old saying: "Showing up is 80 percent of life."

8. CONGRATULATE YOURSELF!

Trail running through the years can be hard work. There will be injuries from which you'll have to recover, as well as the ups and downs of your personal and professional life, which will impact your ability to run. And then there are the inevitable challenges of aging.

But the important thing is that you are out there, still hitting the trails, knocking out those miles! Take a moment to high-five yourself!

It might be that no one has summed up the benefits of trail running as you age better than retired professor Bernd Heinrich, author of **Why We Run**. In the 1980s, Heinrich held a wide range of ultramarathon records. He put it very simply when he wrote, "The essential thing is to run, period. And to do it for a long time, consistently, and then everything takes care of itself."

Keeping It Fun

Stoke is timeless. If you love trail running, it stays with you, somewhere deep in your soul. But that enthusiasm invariably ebbs and flows. The good news is that when you're in a funk, there are a number of simple things you can do to get your groove back. Here are our favorite ways.

1. MIX IT UP A BIT . . .

Seeking out new trails can add spice to your trail running. New trails will take you to new places, allow you to see different scenery, and offer unexpected challenges. But how to find new trails? Ask your running friends. Inquire at a local running store. Pore over maps, looking for those green swaths. Strava heat maps, which show popular trail running routes around the world, are a great resource. Websites and apps like Trail Run Project, AllTrails, and RootsRated can be helpful, too.

When you're running somewhere new, you'll also be altering—however slightly—your distances and style of trail running. That allows your body to adapt to new challenges and develop new strengths. You might even end up running a vertical kilometer or an ultramarathon distance, without even thinking about it!

2. OR MIX IT UP A LOT!

There are all kinds of activities and sports that mix in trail running, including orienteering, triathlons, obstacle races, and even racing with—wait for it!—donkeys.

Orienteering is a sport in which you find hidden locations known as "control points" with a map and compass.

Triathlons are a great way to mix in plenty of cross-training, and try something completely different. And if you don't want to swim, XTERRA duathlons are held throughout the world that include mountain biking and trail running.

Obstacle racing, meanwhile, has been growing. Obstacles might include mud pits, monkey bar traverses, log carries, spear throws, and wall climbs spread out over a 10 km or half-marathon trail running course. They're a lot of fun!

GET YOUR ASS IN GEAR

In 1949 in Leadville, Colorado, a friendly bet between miners about who could "get yer ass over the pass" the quickest led to a fringe sport called burro racing, a crazy pursuit that involves a runner teaming up with a donkey to run a trail race! The races are held in historic mining towns in Colorado. There are about ten races every year, with distances ranging from 4 to 29 miles (6 to 46 km).

3. **RECRUIT A FRIEND—WITH TWO OR FOUR LEGS**

    If you really enjoy trail running, you'll love it even more with friends. Running with friends or joining trail running groups is the best way to share the love. Having a partner for the physical and emotional joys of trail running brings camaraderie, conversation, laughter, and yes, even mutual groans. Trail running with friends can make even a casual 30-minute jog an engaging experience.

    If you can't find a human to share the experience, grab a four-footed sidekick. Dogs love running, love being outdoors, and love doing something with their human companion. For us, that eager canine passion can be positively contagious!

TIPS FOR TRAIL RUNNING WITH YOUR DOG

1. Your dog should be healthy, fit, and at least a year and a half old. All dogs have their limits, but breeds with short muzzles (bulldogs and pugs) are not adept at running longer distances.

2. Start by walking your dog several times on trails you plan to run, so they understand the environment and the process. When you start running, begin with short distances and a gentle pace.

3. Understand and obey dog regulations for the trails you use. Keep your dog on a leash where required, and use voice controls to keep him or her from confronting other trail users. And please, always pick up after your dog!

4. On hot days and during longer runs, make sure to run near freshwater water sources or be ready to share your water. Dogs won't be able to tell you when they're dehydrated.

5. In cold, snowy weather, keep an eye out for excessive ice buildup in your dog's paws. It can lead to injuries and also make your dog unstable on slippery terrain. Some dogs are more susceptible than others to ice buildup. Consider dog booties if this is a problem for your pal.

6. Be careful about running your dog over rocky trails. It can damage their pads if they aren't toughened up.

7. Dogs are fiercely loyal. That's a good thing, most of the time. But it can sometimes lead them to run beyond their limits. Your dog's never going to hold up a sign that says, "On strike! I'm going back to the car."

8. Gear to consider buying for your dog: a lightweight jacket, a leash with elastic tension that you can secure to your waist, doggie energy snacks, portable water bowls, and a GPS collar to help find Fido if he or she is prone to wandering.

9. Want to mix it up with your beast? Try canicross, which is trail racing with your dog! Your dog is attached to you with an elastic lead, and you direct your four-legged partner with voice commands. The activity is growing in popularity, and there are canicross races around the world now.

4. **GIVE IT A REST**

    Not many of us can run five or six days a week for years at a time. So don't hesitate to set aside your trail running and switch gears—especially important at the end of a long, hard season. Not only will your body appreciate it, but when you come back to trail running it will be like meeting an old friend!

5. **CROSS-TRAIN**

    Cross-training is just a fancy way of saying you're doing other sports. Cross-training builds strength, agility, balance, and fitness, often with low-impact activities. Your body will be happier on the days you trail run, you'll have fewer injuries, and you'll find yourself looking forward to trail running, even after a few days off.

6. **CLIMB ON!**

    Push your limits and consider trail running up a high peak. It doesn't have to be Mount Everest—it can be as simple as a small mountain in your corner of the world. Running up a mountain trail—and usually that means power-hiking—can offer a huge sense of satisfaction and reward. Besides, the views are often spectacular and you'll pass hikers who will cheer you on!

7. PLAN A TRAIL RUNNING VACATION

What a planet! There are incredible trails and races all over the place. While the US and Europe have the deepest trail running histories, communities, and races, there are amazing trails to run in just about every country of the world. A few of our favorite places? The Lake District of England, Scotland, the Alps, New Zealand's South Island, and even Iceland!

8. NETFLIX AND CHILL . . . WITH A TRAIL RUNNING MOVIE

There are dozens of inspiring trail running videos available online, for free or dirt cheap. Our favorites: *Leadman: The Dave Mackey Story*, *The Pleasure and the Pain*, *Barkley Number Fifteen*, *Why We Run*, *Sarah Ridgway: Mountain Runner*, *The Lion & The Gazelle*, *A Fine Line*, *Thirty Hours*, *Chasing Walmsley*, and *The Beauty of the Irrational*. Also look for Billy Yang's *15 Hours* series and just about anything from the Salomon TV's Running channel. If that's not enough, search for videos about the world's biggest races like the Ultra-Trail du Mont-Blanc, Western States 100, Hardrock 100, Pikes Peak Marathon, and Jungfrau Marathon. But whatever you watch, start with *That's So Trail*, the funniest trail running video anywhere.

9. BUY NEW KICKS!

NBA basketball star Michael Jordan put on a new pair of shoes each game because he loved how it felt. That's true for us, too—try it! You'll feel as if—all of a sudden—you can fly. While you probably can't bust out a new pair of running shoes for every run, the point here is that you should make sure you don't keep running on your old shoes for too long. Check their wear, note how they feel, and get a new pair every five to six months or after 300 to 500 miles (500 to 800 km).

"*DUM VIVIMUS VIVAMUS.*"

"WHILE WE LIVE, LET US LIVE."

"ISN'T VICTORY BEING ABLE TO PUSH OUR BODIES AND MINDS TO THEIR LIMITS AND, IN DOING SO, DISCOVERING THAT THEY HAVE LED US TO FIND OURSELVES ANEW AND TO CREATE NEW DREAMS?"

—KILIAN JORNET, *RUN OR DIE*

Above all else, when you lace up and head for the door, remember why you trail run. What does it do for you? Is it that flowing feeling of cruising over smooth singletrack? The sense of adventure as you run ridges, splash through rivers, and fly downhill? The enhanced fitness and strength that you get from running on trails?

Remember to always find the beauty that's right out your back door—on your local trails and in your body as it moves through woods and fields. Relish the joy of knowing every single rock, the feeling associated with each turn.

As long as you remind yourself of how lucky you are to have these experiences, every trail run—no matter how mundane— can be a wonderful adventure.

Now go run on a trail.

"IT'S NOT ABOUT THE LEGS; IT'S ABOUT THE HEART AND THE MIND."

—ELIUD KIPCHOGE

269

A Note about COVID

We write this as the world tackles the challenges of the Covid-19 virus. Trail running, too, has been impacted. Before you head out on the trails, please check with your local, regional and national authorities for current best practices so you can trail run safely, protecting both yourself and those around you.

ACKNOWLEDGMENTS

Thanks to all those who lent a hand along the trail, most notably: Mike Ambrose, Stian Angermund, Hadi Barkat, Mike Benge, Emily Geldard, Stephanie Lefferts, Brendan Leonard, Marion Schreiber, Felix Kindelán, Marta Kosinska, Alizée Dabert, Malcolm Pittman, Tayte Pollmann, Max Romey, and Galerie Café des Aiguilles, L'Atelier, and Moody Coffee Roasters, where much of this book was written.

Yitka Winn and Hillary Gerardi, your trail running knowledge and upbeat energy came at just the right moments. Thank you both.

John Anderson, from Tahoe Wilderness Medicine, thanks for being our cutting-edge, thoughtful, go-to resource for all things trail running and medicine. We've learned a lot. Our readers will benefit.

A tip of our snouts to our loyal four-legged trail running partners who have left our sides for more ethereal paths: Barkley, Boggs, Chloe, Rowlf T. Dog, and Samivel. Don't forget to stop at the next junction. In time, we'll be along.

Trail Running Illustrated includes content licensed from *Trail Runner Magazine* that was created by Alex Kurt, Doug Mayer, Randall Levensaler, David Roche, and Yitka Winn.

TRAIL RUNNING ILLUSTRATED

THE ART OF RUNNING FREE

This book was imagined by Doug Mayer, Brian Metzler and Helvetiq.

Text by Doug Mayer, Brian Metzler
Design and layout: Marion Schreiber
Copyeditors: Hadi Barkat, Karin Waldhauser, Laura Larson

ISBN 978-2-940481-89-7
First edition: June 2021
Deposit copy in Switzerland: June 2021

www.helvetiq.com

The book is published in North America by Mountaineers Books.

 MOUNTAINEERS BOOKS is dedicated
to the exploration, preservation, and enjoyment
of outdoor and wilderness areas.

1001 SW Klickitat Way, Suite 201, Seattle, WA 98134
800.553.4453, www.mountaineersbooks.org

Printed in Latvia in June 2021

Library of Congress Cataloging-in-Publication data is on file for this title

Mountaineers Books titles may be purchased for corporate, educational, or
other promotional sales, and our authors are available for a wide range of
events. For information on special discounts or booking an author, contact
our customer service at 800-553-4453 or mbooks@mountaineersbooks.org.

ISBN (paperback): 978-1-68051-566-4
ISBN (ebook): 978-1-68051-567-1

An independent nonprofit publisher since 1960